Trade and Environment: Conflict or Compatibility?

Proceedings of the Royal Institute of International Affairs conference
Chatham House, London, April 1997

Edited by Duncan Brack

THE ROYAL INSTITUTE OF
INTERNATIONAL AFFAIRS
Energy and Environmental Programme
International Economics Programme

EARTHSCAN
Earthscan Publications Ltd, London

First published in Great Britain in 1998 by
Royal Institute of International Affairs, 10 St James's Square, London SW1Y 4LE
(Charity Registration No. 208 223)
and Earthscan Publications Ltd, 120 Pentonville Road, London N1 9JN

Distributed in North America by
The Brookings Institution, 1775 Massachusetts Avenue NW,
Washington DC 20036-2188

Paperback: ISBN 1 85383 577 3

The Royal Institute of International Affairs is an independent body which promotes the
rigorous study of international questions and does not express opinions of its own.
The opinions expressed in this publication are the responsibility of the authors.

Earthscan Publications Limited is an editorially independent subsidiary of Kogan Page Limited
and publishes in association with the International Institute of Environment and Development
and the World Wide Fund for Nature.

Typeset by Koinonia Ltd.
Printed and bound by Biddles Limited, Guildford and King's Lynn
Original cover design by Visible Edge
Cover by Yvonne Booth

Contents

Preface and acknowledgments

Not so long ago, 'international relations' was primarily about security relationships: military alliances, conflicts, stand-offs. The world in the late 1990s is a more complicated place, and nations interact in a rapidly expanding variety of ways. Indeed, individuals and firms increasingly interact with little reference to national governments.

One of the key focal points of international relations in the modern world is international trade, and the rapid dismantling of tariff and non-tariff barriers throughout the world that has driven economic growth and stimulated linkages between activities and communities undreamed of a few decades ago. Another is environmental protection, the growing understanding that many forms of pollution and resource depletion stemming from modern economies pay no respect to national borders and can effectively be tackled only at an inter- or supranational level.

Humans have had hundreds of years to learn how to handle international relations of the traditional sort, but only a few decades to explore the implications of trade liberalization and to develop frameworks of national and international environmental regulation to achieve sustainable development. The two systems are still evolving furiously. Since they have been designed by different people for different – and sometimes conflicting – ends, it is hardly surprising if they sometimes clash.

The trade and environment debate really got going in the early 1990s, when the 'Earth Summit' in Rio, the seemingly endless Uruguay Round negotiations and a series of GATT dispute panel findings on particular trade–environment conflicts all more or less coincided. The new World Trade Organization (WTO), and its Committee on Trade and Environment, was hoped by many to offer a potential resolution of the problem. They were cruelly disappointed by the Committee's report to the first WTO Ministerial Conference in Singapore in December 1996, which was able to conclude little more than that further work was needed. But what the Committee's detailed exchange of views over two years did do was to reveal just how complex this agenda was, involving interconnected webs of trade, environment and development issues and policies that were difficult to separate out and even more difficult to reach consensus over.

This Chatham House conference was the first opportunity for many, participants in the Committee's discussions and interested observers alike, to discuss the state and future of the trade and environment debate: which way after Singapore? These proceedings reproduce the papers (in many cases, expanded beyond what the speakers could deliver in the time available) and a summary of the discussions at the conference.

Chapters reflect the five sessions of the conference. Chapter 1 includes a brief overview of the major issues and the keynote speech, given by one of the main negotiators of the Uruguay Round itself, Sir Leon Brittan. Chapter 2 explores the evidence for the trade and environment conflict: What do trade-related environmental measures seek to do, and how much do they cost? Does international investment avoid host countries with high environmental standards, in a 'race to the bottom'? Chapter 3 presents a wide range of industry concerns, including viewpoints from leading industrial sectors, from developing countries and from others. Chapter 4 examines the legal aspect of the debate: How are trade–environment clashes resolved in the WTO and in the EU? Finally, Chapter 5 draws together key participants from a wide spread of backgrounds to debate the future of the trade–environment debate, of the Committee on Trade and Environment and of international institutions themselves.

Much of the problem in the trade and environment arena, as many conference participants pointed out, is a lack of knowledge, a difference in perceptions and a failure of communication among the different individuals and communities involved. There is no single or final answer to the question 'trade and environment: conflict or compatibility?' But there can be a better understanding of it; and that is the aim of this book.

Acknowledgments

This conference developed originally from an idea by the American Chamber of Commerce (UK), and my sincere thanks go to Robert E. Brunck, its Director-General, and to Don Huss for first stimulating us, and then cooperating with us in its organization. The conference was also convened in association with Cameron May, the leading specialist trade and environment law publisher, and my thanks are due to them.

I am most grateful to the four conference sponsors for providing the financial support that made possible extensive participation from developing countries and NGOs: the UK Department of the Environment, DGI of the European Commission, the Royal Society for the Protection of Birds and Vauxhall Motors. It is one of the strengths of Chatham House, I believe, that it is able to bring together such a diverse range of organizations in support of the cause of spreading knowledge and contributing to understanding.

That objective would not have been so well fulfilled without the contributions from the wide sweep of speakers and conference participants, from governments, industry, NGOs, IGOs and academia, from trade, environment and development backgrounds. I hope I have managed to capture some of the flavour of the wide-ranging discussions that followed the presentations in each of the sessions.

The agenda for the conference was planned over a long period and benefited from insights and input from a wide number of people, many of whom ended up as speakers and participants. I would like to thank in particular James Cameron and Steve Charnovitz for their unending helpfulness in this respect, as in many others. My two programme heads at Chatham House, Michael Grubb and Benn Steil, provided much-needed advice and encouragement.

Finally, the conference could not have happened without the professionalism and hard work of RIIA's Conference Unit, especially Julia Thomas and Philippa Challen; and these proceedings would not be in your hands in such quality without the dedication and skills of RIIA's Publications Department.

April 1998   Duncan Brack

Contributors to the conference

Hussein Abaza, Chief of Environment Unit, United Nations Environment Programme (UNEP)

Charles Arden-Clarke, Policy Coordinator for Trade and Environment, World Wide Fund for Nature (WWF)

Dr Jonathan R. Barton, Senior Research Associate, School of Development Studies, University of East Anglia

Duncan Brack, Senior Research Fellow, Energy and Environmental Programme/ International Economics Programme, Royal Institute of International Affairs

Rt Hon Sir Leon Brittan QC, Vice President of the European Commission; Commissioner responsible for EU trade policy

Robert E. Brunck, Director-General, American Chamber of Commerce (UK)

James Cameron, Director, Foundation for International Environmental Law and Development (FIELD)

John Canning, Eco-Timber Trade Officer, UK Foundation for the South Pacific/ Just World Trading

Dr Damien Geradin, Associate, Coudert Brothers; Senior Research Fellow, Institute for European Legal Studies, University of Liège

Jeffrey L. Gertler, Senior Counsellor, Legal Affairs Division, World Trade Organization

Dr Veena Jha, Economics Affairs Officer, Trade and Environment Section, International Trade Division, United Nations Conference on Trade and Environment (UNCTAD)

Dr James Lee, Director, Trade and Environment Database projects, School of International Service, American University, Washington DC

Dr Reinhard Quick, Head of Liaison Office, Brussels, Verband der Chemischen Industrie eV

Michael Reiterer, Deputy Director-General, Department for European Integration and Trade Policy, Austrian Federal Economic Chamber, Vienna; Co-Chair (Trade), OECD Joint Session of Trade and Environment Experts

Ambassador Juan Carlos Sanchez Arnau, Permanent Representative of Argentina to the UN Office at Geneva and to the WTO/GATT; Chairman, WTO Committee on Trade and Environment 1995–7

Frits Schlingemann, Executive Regional Director, UNEP Regional Office for Europe

William Seddon-Brown, Chairman, EU Committee, American Chamber of Commerce (UK) and European Energy from Waste Coalition

Dr Magda Shahin, Minister Plenipotentiary, Deputy Chief of Mission, Egyptian Mission to the UN Office at Geneva

Sabrina Shaw, Economic Affairs Officer, Trade and Environment, WTO Secretariat

David E. Wakeford, International Trade Manager, Imperial Chemical Industries plc (ICI)

David Wallis, Director, Business Planning and Special Studies, Vauxhall Motors Ltd

Abbreviations

APEC	Asia-Pacific Economic Community
ASEAN	Association of South-East Asian Nations
CAFE	(US) Corporate Average Fuel Economy (regulations)
CFCs	Chlorofluorocarbons
CITES	Convention on International Trade in Endangered Species
CSD	(UN) Commission on Sustainable Development
CTE	(WTO) Committee on Trade and Environment
DPG	Domestically prohibited good
DSB	(WTO) Dispute Settlement Body
DSM	(WTO) Dispute Settlement Mechanism
DSU	(WTO) Dispute Settlement Understanding
ECJ	European Court of Justice
EPA	(US) Environmental Protection Agency
ESCAP	(UN) Economic and Social Commission for Asia and the Pacific
EST	Environmentally sound technology
GATS	General Agreement on Trade in Services
GATT	General Agreement on Tariffs and Trade
GETS	Global Environment and Trade Study
IGO	Intergovernmental organization
IISD	International Institute for Sustainable Development
IPR	Intellectual property right
ISO	International Standards Organization
ITC	International Trade Centre
IUCN	International Union for the Conservation of Nature
LCA	Life-cycle approach
MEA	Multilateral environmental agreement
MFN	Most Favoured Nation
NAFTA	North American Free Trade Agreement
NGO	Nongovernmental organization
NMFS	(US) National Marine Fishing Service
OECD	Organization for Economic Cooperation and Development
PIC	Prior Informed Consent

PPMs	Process and production methods
SMEs	Small and medium-sized enterprizes
SPS	(WTO Agreement on) the Application of Sanitary and Phytosanitary Measures
TBT	(WTO Agreement on) Technical Barriers to Trade
TED	Turtle-excluder device
TNC	Transnational corporation
TREM	Trade-related environmental measure
TRIPS	(WTO Agreement on) Trade-Related Intellectual Property Rights
UNCED	United Nations Conference on Environment and Development
UNCTAD	United Nations Conference on Trade and Development
UNDP	United Nations Development Programme
UNEP	United Nations Environment Programme
USTR	United States Trade Representative
WTO	World Trade Organization

Chapter 1

Introduction: The Trade and Environment Debate

1.1 Guide to the issues[1]
Duncan Brack

Introduction

The gradual evolution of global trade and environmental regimes continues to raise the possibility of conflict. The international community is in theory committed *both* to trade liberalization, through the Uruguay Round extension of the General Agreement on Tariffs and Trade (GATT) and the creation of the World Trade Organization (WTO), *and* to environmentally sustainable development, through the agreements signed at the UN Conference on Environment and Development, the 'Earth Summit' of 1992.

In principle, the pursuit of both objectives should be entirely compatible. According to the theory of comparative advantage, trade allows countries to specialize in the production of goods and services in which they are relatively most efficient. In other words, trade enables countries to maximize output from a given input of resources – which is a movement in the direction of environmental sustainability. Furthermore, trade liberalization can help to remove distortionary subsidies and pricing policies, improving the efficiency of resource allocation, and can encourage the spread of environmentally friendly technology. The higher rate of growth of income resulting from trade also helps to generate the resources needed for investment in environmental protection – although this is not an automatic link, and appropriate policies need to be pursued simultaneously.

---

[1] This paper was originally printed as Royal Institute of International Affairs Briefing Paper 35 (February 1997): *Trade and Environment: An Update on the Issues.*

Given modern systems of economic activity, however, trade can also harm the environment. To the extent that environmental externalities are not incorporated in economic prices and decision-making, trade can act to magnify unsustainable patterns of economic activity, exacerbating problems of pollution and resource depletion. Where externalities are being incorporated (through environmental taxation, for example, or regulation), the process is invariably proceeding at different speeds in different countries. Yet trade rules are set internationally, and the multilateral trading system (the complex of agreements centred around the GATT and administered by the WTO) may fail to allow for such differences in national efforts at achieving environmental sustainability, even when policies are aimed at controlling transboundary or global environmental problems. In addition, a country with strict environmental regulations may fear that its economy will be undermined by competition from other countries with more lax environmental standards (and hence potentially lower production costs).

Trade and environmental policies are therefore inextricably interlinked. Conflict between trade liberalization and environmental protection has already erupted in a number of instances as regulations drawn up in pursuit of the objective of environmental sustainability have been challenged as erecting barriers to trade, notably in several cases brought before disputes panels of the GATT and WTO. The very first dispute under the WTO (which went through both a panel and the Appellate Body) was on a trade–environment case. The WTO itself, on its creation on 1 January 1995, established a Committee on Trade and Environment (CTE), taking forward the work carried out in the former GATT Working Group on Environmental Measures and International Trade (formally created in 1971 but inactive until 1991). Its aim is 'to identify the relationship between trade measures and environmental measures, in order to promote sustainable development', and 'to make appropriate recommendations on whether any modifications of the provisions of the multilateral trading system are required …'.[2] The Committee reported to the first WTO Ministerial Meeting in Singapore in December 1996, and had its mandate renewed; aspects of its discussions and conclusions are highlighted below.

---

[2] WTO: Trade and Environment Decision of 14 April 1994 (see Box 1.1 for extracts).

Many other international organizations, including the OECD, the UN Environment Programme (UNEP), the UN Conference on Trade and Development (UNCTAD) and a large number of academic institutes and NGOs, have also published work in the area. Two new organizations were established during 1996: the International Panel on Trade, Environment and Sustainable Development, established by the World Wide Fund for Nature and sponsored by a number of European governments; and the Geneva-based International Centre for Trade and Sustainable Development, supported by the International Union for the Conservation of Nature.

This paper aims to provide an outline of the major issues involved in the trade and environment debate.

Use of trade measures for environmental purposes

The central aim of the GATT is to liberalize trade between contracting parties. Article I ('most favoured nation' treatment) requires that any trade advantage granted by any contracting party to any product either for import or export must also be applied to any 'like product' originating in or bound for any other contracting party. Article III ('national treatment') similarly requires imported and domestic 'like products' to be treated identically with respect to internal taxes and regulations. WTO members, in other words, are not permitted to discriminate between other WTO members' traded products, or between domestic and international production.

The GATT does, however, permit certain unilateral trade restrictions in the pursuit of environmental protection under particular circumstances. Article XX ('General Exceptions') states that: ⊄ p.73

> Subject to the requirement that such measures are not applied in a manner which would constitute a means of arbitrary or unjustifiable discrimination between countries where the same conditions prevail, or a disguised restriction on international trade, nothing in this Agreement shall be construed to prevent the adoption or enforcement by any contracting party of measures:
>
> . . .
>
> (b) necessary to protect human, animal or plant life or health;
>
> . . .

Box 1.1: World Trade Organization – Trade and Environment Decision of 14 April 1994 (extracts)

Ministers,

Meeting on the occasion of signing the Final Act embodying the results of the Uruguay Round of Multilateral Trade Negotiations at Marrakesh on 15 April 1994,

...

Decide:

– to direct the first meeting of the General Council of the WTO to establish a Committee on Trade and Environment open to all members of the WTO to report to the first biennial meeting of the Ministerial Conference after the entry into force of the WTO when the work and terms of reference of the Committee will be reviewed, in the light of recommendations of the Committee,

– that the TNC Decision of 15 December 1993 which reads, in part, as follows:

'(a) to identify the relationship between trade measures and environmental measures, in order to promote sustainable development;

(b) to make appropriate recommendations on whether any modifications of the provisions of the multilateral trading system are required, compatible with the open equitable and non-discriminatory nature of the system, as regards, in particular:

– the need for rules to enhance positive interaction between trade and environmental measures, for the promotion of sustainable development, with special consideration to the needs of developing countries, in particular those of the least developed among them; and

– the avoidance of protectionist trade measures, and the adherence to effective multilateral disciplines to ensure responsiveness of the multilateral trading system to environmental objectives set forth in Agenda 21 and the Rio Declaration, in particular Principle 12; and

– surveillance of trade measures used for environmental purposes, of trade-related aspects of environmental measures which have significant trade effects, and of effective implementation of the multilateral disciplines governing those measures;'

constitutes, along with the preambular language above, the terms of reference of the Committee on Trade and Environment,

(g) relating to the conservation of exhaustible natural resources if such measures are made effective in conjunction with restrictions on domestic production or consumption.

Countries can, therefore, ban or restrict the import of products that will harm their own environments, as long as the standards applied are non-discriminatory between countries and between domestic and foreign production. Environmental grounds have indeed become more widely cited as an objective and rationale for applying trade-restrictive regulations including, most notably, measures aimed at controlling air pollution and

> – that, within these terms of reference, and with the aim of making international trade and environmental policies mutually supportive, the Committee will initially address the following matters, in relation to which any relevant issue may be raised:
>
> > – the relationship between the provisions of the multilateral trading system and trade measures for environmental purposes, including those pursuant to multilateral environmental agreements;
> >
> > – the relationship between environmental policies relevant to trade and environmental measures with significant trade effects and the provisions of the multilateral trading system;
> >
> > – the relationship between the provisions of the multilateral trading system and:
> >
> > > (a) charges and taxes for environmental purposes;
> > >
> > > (b) requirements for environmental purposes relating to products, including standards and technical regulations, packaging, labelling and recycling;
> >
> > – the provisions of the multilateral trading system with respect to the transparency of trade measures used for environmental purposes and environmental measures and requirements which have significant trade effects;
> >
> > – the relationship between the dispute settlement mechanisms in the multilateral trading system and those found in multilateral environmental agreements;
> >
> > – the effect of environmental measures on market access, especially in relation to developing countries, in particular to the least developed among them, and environmental benefits of removing trade restrictions and distortions;
> >
> > – the issue of exports of domestically prohibited goods,
>
> – that the Committee on Trade and Environment will consider the work programme envisaged in the Decision on Trade in Services and the Environment and the relevant provisions of the Agreement on Trade-Related Aspects of Intellectual Property Rights as an integral part of its work, within the above terms of reference . . .

hazardous chemicals.[3] Any agreement permitting a restriction in trade, however, runs the risk of capture by protectionist interests using environmental justification as a disguise. To that end, the CTE spent some time discussing transparency requirements for such measures. The Uruguay Round agreement incorporated many improvements in the requirements for notification of measures under the Agreements on Technical Barriers to Trade (TBT), Sanitary and Phytosanitary Measures, and Subsidies and Countervailing Measures. While considering that no further modifications

---

[3] *International Trade 1990–91* (Geneva: GATT Secretariat, 1992), p. 32.

to WTO rules were necessary, the CTE concluded that the establishment of a central database of trade-related environmental measures would be helpful. Relatively little analysis has in fact been carried out on the impact of such measures, but at least one study has concluded that they are relatively inexpensive, tend to be short-term and are often well worth the cost in terms of environmental benefits[4] (see further in Section 2.2).

Product requirements

Generally speaking, environmental regulations apply either to products or to processes. Product requirements, as well as outright bans, include regulations and/or voluntary agreements governing labelling, packaging, recycling and recycled content. Increasingly, such requirements are based on life-cycle assessments of the product's environmental impact during production, consumption and disposal. Although these can be valuable instruments of environmental policy, the application of such requirements to imported products can pose significant difficulties. Information, particularly in life-cycle assessment cases, may be wholly or partially lacking. Characteristics chosen for labelling may reflect domestic environmental priorities, and criteria used in different national schemes may vary widely. Schemes that focus only on particular products (e.g. tropical timber) may create artificial advantages for products that are not subject to similar requirements (e.g. temperate timber or substitutes such as plastics or metals) but whose consumption and production nevertheless have environmental impact. Packaging regulations that require recovery and reuse (e.g. returnable bottles) clearly create problems for non-domestic producers. Foreign governments and industries are highly unlikely to be involved in designing and implementing such schemes. Not only do these problems combine to create barriers to trade (particularly for developing countries), but they may also lead to resource misallocation and potentially inappropriate environmental policies.

---

[4] James Lee, Antonio Santiago, Ali Ghobaldi and Roland Mollerus, 'Trade-Related Environmental Measures: Sizing and Comparing Impacts' (Global Environment and Trade Study, June 1996).

The TBT Agreement aims to ensure that regulations such as these do not create unnecessary obstacles to international trade; environmental protection is singled out as a legitimate objective of technical requirements and standards. The Agreement requires, *inter alia*, that all such measures should be as transparent as possible and based on international standards where feasible. The CTE, which spent most of its time under this item discussing voluntary ecolabelling schemes, stressed the importance of sticking to the Agreement's provisions and ensuring fair access to foreign producers. It is unclear, however, whether recycling and waste management requirements, and labelling schemes incorporating information about production processes, are covered by the Agreement, and the CTE resolved to consider these issues further. The OECD has proposed a series of steps to minimize disruption to trade, including transparency; transitional adaptation periods; sensitivity to non-domestic conditions and particularly to the special needs of developing countries and economies in transition; greater harmonization of life-cycle methodologies; and a requirement for genuine environmental justification for all such measures.[5]

A specific issue related to the trade in products is the export of *domestically prohibited goods*. Goods that are restricted in domestic markets, on the grounds that they present a danger to human, animal or plant life or health, or to the environment, may often be legally exported. This may cause a problem for the importing country, where information is lacking on whether and why the product is banned: exporters may make false declarations, customs authorities (particularly in developing countries) may lack adequate product testing facilities, and undeveloped or ineffective consumer protection legislation may, for example, enable products to be marketed beyond their expiry dates. Trade in hazardous waste is covered by the Basel Convention, and the negotiation of further multilateral environmental agreements (MEAs) may prove the best way to make progress on this issue. A legal requirement for 'prior informed consent' for export is increasingly common within the European Union (for example

---

[5] See *Report on Trade and Environment to the OECD Council at Ministerial Level* (Paris: OECD, 1995).

for the export of restricted chemicals) and this may also provide a way forward. As with many other trade–environment topics, transparency of measures, and the provision of technical assistance to developing countries, are key issues.

Process and production methods

Environmental regulations based on process and production *methods* (PPMs), as opposed to *product* standards, cause more complex interactions with trade. Although the GATT's 'like product' provisions were not drawn up with environmental issues in mind, a GATT dispute panel applied them in the case of the well-known US–Mexico tuna-dolphin dispute in 1991. It ruled that the trade restriction in question (the US import ban on Mexican tuna caught with dolphin-unfriendly nets) was in breach of the GATT because it discriminated against a product on the basis of the way in which it was produced, not on the basis of its own characteristics; i.e., it discriminated against a 'like product'.

The meaning of 'like product' has become one of the most difficult issues in the trade–environment arena. In 1994 another GATT panel, ruling on an EU–US dispute over car imports, slightly relaxed the definition, considering that vehicles of different fuel efficiency standards could be considered *not* to be like products. However, it placed strict boundaries on this conclusion, arguing that Article III of the GATT referred only to a 'product as a product, from its introduction into the market to its final consumption'.[6] Factors relating to the manufacture of the product before its introduction into the market were, therefore, still irrelevant. Another panel in 1996 found that chemically identical imported and domestic gasoline were like products regardless of the environmental standards of the producers.[7]

Even if one does not adopt the panels' viewpoints, PPM-based environmental trade measures can be difficult to justify. Different parts of the world vary widely in their ability to assimilate pollution, depending on factors such as climate, population density, existing levels of pollution and

---

[6] US: Taxes on Automobiles, Report of the Panel (1994), para. 5.52.
[7] US: Standards for Reformulated and Conventional Gasoline (1996).

risk preferences. Environmental regulations suited to industrialized nations, with high population densities and environments that have been subject to pollution for the past 200 years, may be wholly inappropriate for newly industrializing countries with much lower population densities and inherited pollution levels – and yet trade measures based on PPMs could in effect seek to impose the higher standards regardless. Carried to its logical extreme, enforcing similarity of PPMs could deny the very basis of comparative advantage, which rests on the proposition that countries possess different cost structures for the production of various goods. It is hardly surprising that many developing countries view the motives of those wishing to introduce this issue to the debate as protectionist. Another argument rests on practicalities. By their very nature, PPMs cannot generally be determined by inspection of the products. Importers wishing to apply PPM-based controls must therefore enjoy the cooperation of the exporting country or country of origin in certifying how the goods are produced.

PPM-based measures are, however, becoming increasingly important in strategies for environmental sustainability. Particularly where the use of energy is involved (as it is in virtually every manufacturing and processing activity), the pollution caused stems from the PPM and not the product. Life-cycle approaches have similarly focused attention on the way in which products are manufactured, grown and harvested, as well on product characteristics themselves. In terms of trade measures, an important distinction can be drawn between PPMs that cause pollution that is restricted to the country of production, and those that cause pollution that is transboundary or global. In the latter case, differentiating, as the panels' interpretation of the GATT effectively does, between pollution associated with the *consumption* of a product and that associated with its *production* is more difficult to justify, and would rule out any trade measure aimed at protecting a country's environment, or any aspect of the global commons, from damage caused by transboundary pollution originating from production.

Inclusion of PPM-based trade measures in MEAs may provide a solution, and in fact the Montreal Protocol (on ozone-depleting substances) includes provision for such measures, though they have not so far been deployed. The OECD has accepted that in some cases PPM-based trade restrictions may have a place in MEAs. Recognizing the difficulties involved in determining the PPMs used from physical inspection of the product, it has called for the development of verification and certification systems and for the mutual recognition of such systems.

The negotiation of international treaties is frequently, however, a difficult and slow process. A number of participants in the debate[8] have therefore called for the GATT to be amended to set out objective criteria under which trade measures directed against PPMs could be taken (including requirements such as non-discriminatory and transparent measures and evidence of significant transboundary environmental problems), subject to challenge under normal GATT rules. This issue does not feature explicitly on the agenda of the CTE, but underlies many other areas of concern, and is likely to feature increasingly in trade disputes. Recent debates over actual or potential trade restrictions against fur caught in leghold traps, genetically engineered maize and shrimps fished by methods that kill sea turtles all focus attention on processes, not products.

Economic instruments

Economic instruments – taxes and charges, tradeable permits, deposit refund systems and subsidies – are playing an increasingly important role in environmental policy as complements to regulatory instruments and voluntary agreements. In principle, they aim to ensure that environmental externalities are incorporated in decision-making, and in general they are more efficient and more transparent than simple regulatory measures.

The WTO agreements already cover to a certain extent the impact of economic instruments on trade. *Subsidies* are dealt with in the Agreement on Subsidies and Countervailing Measures, which permits government assistance to promote the adaptation of existing facilities to new environmental requirements, as long as this is limited to 20% of the cost.

WTO members are permitted to adjust *tax rates* at the border – i.e. to

[8] See in particular Paul Ekins, *Harnessing Trade to Sustainable Development* (Oxford: Green College, 1995), pp. 10–11; and Natural Resources Defense Council/Foundation for International Environmental Law and Development, *Environmental Priorities for the World Trading System* (Washington DC: NRDC, 1995), p. 9.

impose taxes on imports and rebate taxes on exports so that domestic producers and exporters are not undercut by foreign producers – inasmuch as these are applied to traded *products*. Following the discussion on PPMs above, it would appear that taxes and charges related to processes and production methods cannot be so adjusted, though the GATT is not completely clear on this and a Working Party on Border Tax Adjustments in 1970 failed to draw any conclusion on so-called *taxes occultes* (consumption taxes on materials and services used in the production and transport of other goods).[9] The 1987 GATT dispute panel on the US Superfund regulations ruled that import taxes applied to certain chemicals *and to derivatives of them* were permissible, since US chemicals and derivatives were subject to similar taxes. It has been argued that the same case can be made for energy consumed in the production process, and that border tax adjustments for carbon or energy taxes should therefore be permissible. In fact, the Subsidies Agreement explicitly provides for special treatment for rebating indirect taxes on energy, fuels and oils used in the production process for *exports*.

There are, however, very severe problems involved with the practicalities of border tax adjustments, including the valuation of the appropriate level of tax, the likely wide diversity in national tax rates (given, as noted above, that environmental costs vary not only with products and processes but also with location) and the difficulty of verifying PPM-based damage from an inspection of products. The CTE undertook only a preliminary examination of some of the issues in this complex and controversial topic, and called for further work.

Multilateral environmental agreements

As Principle 12 of the Rio Declaration states, international agreement is clearly preferable to unilateral action in tackling transboundary or global environmental problems. More than 180 MEAs already exist, of which about 20 incorporate trade measures. These include three of the most

---

[9] For a full discussion, see Steve Charnovitz, 'Free Trade, Fair Trade, Green Trade: Defogging the Debate', Cornell International Law Journal, 27:3 (1994), pp. 498–505.

important: the Basel Convention on hazardous waste, the Convention on International Trade in Endangered Species (CITES) and the Montreal Protocol on ozone-depleting substances. In the absence of any comprehensive framework of global environmental law, the negotiation of further MEAs – such as the Kyoto Protocol to the Climate Change Convention – will form an increasingly prominent part of the international agenda.

On the face of it, however, there would appear to be some conflict between current GATT rules and MEAs that contain trade provisions. The Montreal Protocol, for instance, permits parties to ban imports of chlorofluorocarbons and other controlled substances from non-parties, which breaches the 'most favoured nation' and 'national treatment' clauses of GATT. It is widely accepted, however, that the inclusion of this measure in the Montreal Protocol has contributed significantly to its success in attracting signatories,[10] and future MEAs may similarly benefit from the inclusion of trade restrictions.

This topic became one of the most important items of debate on the CTE, with members putting forward proposals designed variously to define under what conditions trade measures taken pursuant to an MEA could be considered to be 'necessary' under the terms of the GATT's Article XX, or to establish a degree of WTO oversight on the negotiation and operation of trade provisions in future MEAs.[11] No consensus was reached about the need for modifications to trade rules. The CTE noted, however, that:

> Trade measures based on specifically agreed-upon provisions can also be needed in certain cases to achieve the environmental objectives of an MEA, particularly where trade is related directly to the source of an environmental problem. They have played an important role in some MEAs in the past, and they may be needed to play a similarly important role in certain cases in the future.[12]

---

[10] See Duncan Brack, *International Trade and the Montreal Protocol* (London: RIIA/ Earthscan, 1996) for a full discussion.
[11] For a good analysis (from an environmental point of view), see World Wide Fund for Nature, *Trade Measures and Multilateral Environmental Agreements: Backwards or Forwards in the WTO?* (Gland, Switzerland: WWF, 1996).
[12] *Report of the Committee on Trade and Environment* (1996), para. 173.

The Committee also recognized that a range of provisions in the WTO can already accommodate the use of trade measures in MEAs; these include the provisions of Article XX, and also of Article XXV, which permits the waiver of other GATT provisions, though on case-by-case and time-limited bases. NGOs have tended to argue for amendment to the GATT to create a presumption of compatibility with MEAs.[13] It is worth noting, however, that no complaint has yet arisen within the GATT or WTO with respect to trade measures taken in pursuit of an MEA, and this may well continue to be the case; in instances such as the Montreal Protocol, where the trade provisions were designed to encourage countries to accede, this has been so successful that there are virtually no non-parties left against whom trade measures could be taken in any case.

Environmental policy, market access and the removal of trade distortions

In what is probably the only area of broad consensus, it is generally agreed that the ending of economically distortionary practices such as subsidies for agriculture or energy would benefit both trade (improving allocative efficiency) and the environment (removing support for environmentally unsustainable activities). Similarly, ending the practice of tariff escalation, by which developing countries face higher tariffs against exports of manufactured and processed goods than for raw materials and primary products (common particularly in the timber and wood products sector), would encourage economic diversification and help end environmentally damaging systems of resource extraction. The GATT Uruguay Round made progress on this issue in the areas of agriculture and textiles, where the system of quotas on developing-country exports known as the Multi-Fibre Arrangement is due to be phased out over a ten-year period. CTE discussions on this item focused in particular on the needs of countries that are currently marginal participants in world trade, and on small and medium-sized enterprizes.

---

[13] See e.g. NRDC/FIELD, *Environmental Priorities for the World Trading System*, p. 17.

International competitiveness

The impact of environmental regulation on economic competitiveness is much debated. Firms in countries with high environmental standards and costs of compliance may fear that they will be undercut by competition from companies based in countries with less strict regulation and lower costs. In theory, this may lead to entire industries departing for countries with lower standards, the so-called 'pollution havens'. Solutions that have been advocated in order to avoid a general lowering of environmental standards include the equalization of costs through countervailing duties. The purpose of these measures (sometimes referred to 'ecodumping' duties or 'ecoduties') is to level the playing field by ensuring that products imported from countries with lower environmental standards are subject to duties or tariffs to offset the implicit subsidy they enjoy from lower environmental costs.

In practice, however, there does not appear to be much evidence for industrial migration. For most industries, costs attributable to environmental regulations rarely exceed about 1.5% of the total. Countries with initially low environmental standards are not immune to pressures to raise them. Indeed, it can be argued that, in a dynamic business environment, higher environmental standards may in practice act as a spur to innovation and competitive success. Trade may be a key factor in the ratcheting-*up* of standards, as manufacturers seek to expand markets for the products they are required to produce for countries with the higher standards. Nevertheless, it has been argued that concerns over competitiveness may become more relevant as the costs of environmental compliance rise, particularly for sectors such as energy-intensive manufacturing and processing.

Unsurprisingly, this topic does not feature in the work programme of the CTE. Although it could be argued that a failure to incorporate environmental costs is equivalent to an implicit subsidy, and should be countervailable under GATT's Article VI if the subsidized imports cause material damage to domestic production, the Subsidies Agreement carefully defines a subsidy as 'a financial contribution by a government or any public body'[14] – i.e. *not* an implicit subsidy arising from lower environmental

---

[14] Agreement on Subsidies and Countervailing Measures, Article 1.1(a)(1).

standards. Even ignoring this, the concept of ecoduties raises many practical problems, including the appropriateness of the standards being defended, the danger of capture by protectionist interests, the possible removal of competitive pressures on domestic industry and the ever-present fear of retaliation.

The practical problems of border tax adjustment have been considered above. Nevertheless, some participants in the debate[15] have argued that it may be necessary to contemplate countervailing duties to defuse industrial opposition to higher environmental standards and to prevent concerns that loss of competitiveness may become a significant drag on environmental legislation. The OECD, while affirming its opposition to countervailing duties, considered that further research on the extent of the problem would be helpful.

Dispute settlement

The World Trade Organization's Disputes Settlement Understanding established a unified system which applies to all WTO agreements. It operates to stricter time limits and is more transparent than the GATT system it replaced, and the findings of disputes panels are adopted automatically by WTO members unless they decide by consensus other-wise: the reverse of the pre-Uruguay Round position. The Understanding also enables panels to request written advisory reports from expert groups, and CTE members have underlined the importance of following this procedure in areas of trade–environment interaction – while recognizing that it is not within the mandate of panels to question the merits of national or international environmental objectives. In general, it is believed that the new system is a considerable improvement on the old, and panel findings have certainly been published much more speedily than before. CTE discussions largely concentrated on the interaction between WTO and MEA disputes settlement mechanisms but, as with the wider question, failed to reach any conclusion.

---

[15] Ekins, *Harnessing Trade to Sustainable Development*, p. 17.

Conclusion

The trade–environment debate is not going to go away. On the contrary, the combination of the growth in trade anticipated from the implementation of the Uruguay Round agreements and the accumulating evidence of global environmental degradation, together with the pressure for international action that will result, seems likely to lead to more, and more serious, conflicts. Set against this background, the findings of the first report of the World Trade Organization's Committee on Trade and Environment – which were little more than that more work was needed – were a disappointment to many.

It may be, however, that the CTE will never be able to conclude very much by itself. The GATT/WTO regime tends to progress through negotiating 'rounds' (such as the Uruguay Round, the most recent) covering a very broad sweep of topics; trade-offs are then possible which ensure that every participant benefits directly from at least some of the elements of the final package. It may be that progress on the trade–environment issue will have to wait until the next WTO round, for which there are already calls.[16]

More fundamentally, it may be that the WTO by itself, even in the context of a new trade round, will not be able to resolve the trade–environment conflict. One of the problems inherent in this issue is that debates are conducted within, but rarely between, two separate communities, each encompassing governments, international organizations, NGOs and businesses: those motivated by trade liberalization and those motivated by environmental protection. These two groups of people possess different assumptions, values and modes of operating, and tend to lack a full understanding and appreciation of each other's position.

Where the two sides can be brought together – as they can, for instance, within the European Union, where the European Court of Justice is enabled to strike a balance in disputes between the two Treaty of Rome objectives of trade and environment – then the pursuit of their two objectives can be

---

[16] The UK government has argued for the launch of a new multilateral round before 2000, to be concluded and implemented no later than 2010; see *Free Trade and Foreign Policy: A Global Vision*, Cm. 3437 (London: HMSO, November 1996), p. 30.

brought into harmony. Further research and analysis, joint discussion and open debate are the prerequisites for progress in resolving the conflicts inherent in the pursuit of trade liberalization and environmental protection.

Box 1.2: Further references

In addition to the documents referred to in the footnotes, readers may find the following of interest:

Duncan Brack, 'Balancing trade and the environment', *International Affairs*, 71:3 (July 1995).

James Cameron, Paul Demaret and Damien Geradin (eds), *Trade and Environment: The Search for Balance* (London: Cameron May, 1994). (Cameron May also publishes *International Trade Law Reports*, reprinting WTO panel findings, together with a commentary, as they occur.)

Steve Charnovitz, 'GATT and the environment: examining the issues' *International Environmental Affairs*, 4:3 (Summer 1992).

Dan Esty, *Greening the GATT: Trade, Environment and the Future* (Washington DC: Institute for International Economics, 1994).

Global Environment and Trade Study web site (http://www.igc.apc.org/gets) contains links to other trade and environment resources, as well as much useful material of its own. (GETS is a collaborative enterprise involving the Foundation for International Environmental Law and Development, Yale University Center for Environmental Law and Policy and the US Institute of Agriculture and Trade Policy.)

House of Commons Environment Committee, World Trade and the Environment (London: HMSO, HC149, June 1996).

International Centre for Trade and Sustainable Development web site (http://www.ictsd.org) contains much useful trade and environment material, including in particular the *BRIDGES Weekly Trade News Digest* and *BRIDGES Monthly Trade Review*.

Robert Repetto, *Trade and Sustainable Development* (Geneva: UNEP, 1994). (This is the first of the UNEP 'Environment and Trade' series of booklets.)

1.2 Trade and environment after Singapore
Leon Brittan

The programme of this conference clearly demonstrates that the inter-action between trade and environment is indeed an issue that raises some complex questions about how the drive towards trade liberalization interacts with equally laudable environmental policy aims. At Marrakesh in 1994 and at Singapore in 1996, the growing recognition globally that an open trading system is one of the key motors of economic growth coincided with the awareness that we all share a crucial interest in the protection of the global environment. The relationship, or, to put it in the terms of the conference, 'the conflict or compatibility', between trade and environment is, therefore, an issue that evokes interest well beyond professional trade circles and is important for the credibility and reputation of the multilateral trading system. Different players bring different perceptions. Industry worries about competitiveness. How can they compete efficiently and fairly when countries impose different levels of environmental protection or introduce their own labelling require-ments? Environmental activists worry about the impact of the multilateral trading system on the environment. Will not the increased economic activity that flows from freer trade further degrade the environment and add intolerable pressure to the exploitation of natural resources? Developing countries worry about the impact of the debate on their economies. Will they face the imposition of environmental standards designed to meet the concerns of more affluent societies?

These and other questions come together in the debate on trade and environment and were discussed in depth in the WTO Committee on Trade and Environment, the CTE. The issues are complex, so that it may sometimes be frustrating – but should not be surprising – that they are still a long way from being resolved.

Before entering into the results and achievements so far of the WTO discussions, I would like to set the framework and point out what I would regard as the four basic issues in the trade and environment debate.

First, will the economic boost imparted by freer trade lead to increased environmental damage? I would argue that trade, in itself, does not cause environmental harm. A more open trading system can actually bring benefits to the environment. This is because an open trading system encourages the production of commodities and goods where the competitive advantage is greatest. Open trade encourages efficient production, which is by its nature less demanding on the environment. This understanding is crucial to the concept of sustainable development as articulated by the UN Conference on Environment and Development in Rio de Janeiro in 1992. Trade and economic growth are not incompatible with high environmental standards, but obviously the higher standards do not come into existence of themselves. Economic growth can put increased pressure on the environment and has then to be absorbed in an acceptable way through appropriate environmental policies at national and international levels.

The second key issue arises from the relationship between environmental protection and competitiveness. There are understandable concerns that higher environmental standards in one country lend competitive advantage to another. Logical as this may seem at first sight, there is to my knowledge no real evidence so far to suggest that high environmental standards are indeed a key factor in location decisions or have led to large-scale relocation of industry. This is not surprising, since environmental requirements typically represent only between 1% and 2% of overall production costs in the European Union. Moreover, a too simplistic analysis would probably ignore that there is in fact a growing demand for environmentally friendly products. This market is growing at a rate of approximately 8% per year. None the less, the effects of environmental standards on the competitiveness of companies and their investment decisions remain a crucial element in the debate.

Different environmental standards are a reflection of different national priorities and needs. There is no automatic scale of environmental protection that can be applied universally, and it is a fundamental principle that countries have the right to make their own judgments on the standards that they apply.

This brings me to my third basic issue. Setting environmental standards within a territory may be fine; but what about damage that spills over national borders? In a rapidly globalizing world, more and more of these problems cannot be effectively solved at the national or bilateral level, or even at the level of regional trading blocs like the European Union. Global problems require global solutions, and therefore we should all applaud the important progress that has been made through so-called multilateral environmental agreements, such as the Montreal Protocol on ozone-depleting substances, the Convention on International Trade in Endangered Species and the Basel Convention on transboundary movements of hazardous waste. This also means that unilateral action should be avoided. At best it will lead to a piecemeal approach. At worst it will drown the solution to environmental problems in a confusion of tit-for-tat measures, mutual recrimination and misunderstanding. I am firmly convinced that solutions can and should be found through the conclusion of multilateral or bilateral agreements.

The fourth and final key issue of the debate is the interaction between the rules of the world trading system and the instruments to protect the environment. The first point to make in this regard is that the rules of the WTO place very little constraint on the ability of members to devise and implement environmental policies for their own territories. As long as they are not discriminatory against imported products, there is in fact wide latitude for measures to control domestic production systems or the consumption of environmentally damaging goods. Moreover, the original GATT texts made explicit allowance in Article XX for trade measures that are deemed necessary to protect human, animal or plant health or which relate to the conservation of exhaustible natural resources. The acknowledgment of environmental objectives was further confirmed in the preamble to the WTO Agreement by reference to the objective of sustainable development.

Having said this, I have no intention of painting too rosy a picture of the present position. There is in fact a clear need for clarification of the relationship between the rules of the WTO and environmental goals. The European Union was one of the first to recognize this and it sought improvements to Article XX to expand the scope for trade action for environmental purposes, an issue to which I will come back later.

The work of the CTE started in 1995 after the conclusion of the Uruguay Round at Marrakesh. It is no secret that certain WTO members, and in particular the developing countries led by India and Brazil, were reluctant to inject the environmental dimension into the new institution and to create an 'environmental window' in the WTO. As I pointed out earlier, a large group of WTO members regard this process with some suspicion and fear that it will be used for 'green' protectionism by their wealthier trading partners. In order to persuade these countries to participate fully in the CTE, the number of issues on the CTE work programme had to be increased. As a counterweight to the issues sponsored by the European Union and the United States, other problems such as market access, trade liberalization in agriculture and intellectual property rights, where the interaction with environmental protection is much more remote, also had to be put on the agenda of the CTE and were discussed at great length during the 13 meetings that were held in 1995 and 1996.

The work of the CTE was therefore structured around ten items, and the European Union has been particularly active on items 1 (multilateral environment agreements and WTO rules), 3b (ecolabelling) and 6 (impact of environmental measures on market access and environmental benefits of removing trade restrictions and distortions). The Union's role was not, however, limited to those points. Indeed, we played a leading role in the Committee's discussions over the last two years and our approach was very ambitious. All along we tried to obtain concrete results for the Singapore Ministerial Conference of the WTO in December 1996.

On item 1 (MEAs) we submitted a proposal for a new approach on the relationship between MEAs and the rules of the WTO. We suggested amendments to Article XX of the GATT, making, for example, an explicit reference to 'environment' in Article XX(b) or, alternatively, providing an understanding establishing some sort of special treatment for trade measures taken under MEAs by virtue of which these measures would not have to pass the strict 'necessity test' of Article XX. This work was guided by the assumption that the WTO should, as a matter of principle, be supportive of action at the multilateral level for the protection of the environment. Unfortunately, it was not possible to find consensus on our idea to modify WTO rules on these points. We have, however, been able to resist strong pressure to move away from the status quo and to introduce additional disciplines, going beyond the ones provided for in the present GATT Article XX. Attempts were in fact made to push through a set of guidelines concerning the use of trade measures under MEAs which would have included criteria such as proportionality and least trade restrictiveness. Had these attempts been successful, it would have become more difficult to justify trade measures taken under MEAs, under the rules of the WTO. We successfully averted these attempts, and the final CTE report states, albeit in a careful manner, that the WTO is supportive of action at the multilateral level in order to address transboundary and global environmental problems.

The Union has also pressed hard for recognition by the WTO rules of voluntary ecolabelling schemes based on the life-cycle approach (LCA). Our view has always been, and still is, that labelling is a low-cost and transparent means of informing an increasingly discerning consumer about the environmental acceptability of a product. These schemes need not be an inhibition to the free flow of trade, since they are voluntary and do not result in trade barriers if they are non-discriminatory and transparent. Many WTO members, however, opposed our interpretation and expressed the view that the use of criteria relating to process and production methods (PPMs), which are an integral part of labelling based on the life-cycle approach, is not compatible with WTO rules or with the Technical Barriers to Trade (TBT) code in particular. They argued that the principle of national treatment, in connection with the concept of 'like products', does not allow the application to imported products of criteria that are not related to their physical characteristics or their performance. The final CTE report, however, while leaving this intricate legal question undecided, pays tribute to the usefulness and desirability of ecolabelling schemes. As I see it, this will allow us to claim a recognition under the TBT code or under a code of conduct of these schemes.

Another subject on the CTE's agenda which received particular attention by the European Union is item 6, on the relationship between trade liberalization and environmental protection. Here the main objective of the EU has been to obtain WTO recognition that specific measures may be taken to accompany trade liberalization when this is necessary to protect the environment. Discussions in the CTE on this topic focused on the reluctance of developing countries to accept any kind of recognition of the need to implement sustainable development and effective environmental policies. Similarly, the Cairns Group [comprising 15 major agricultural exporting countries] tried to concentrate the CTE's deliberations on agriculture and the environment in an attempt to prepare the ground for the review of the WTO Agreement on Agriculture. The final report stresses that trade liberalization will on the whole generate positive environmental effects, but also indicates that these benefits are by no means automatic. It sends out a clear signal that accompanying environmental measures are allowed when necessary to ensure the achievement of sustainable development. This was one of the main 'green' messages contained in the Commission Communication to the Council of early 1996 on Trade and Environment, and in our view the outcome in the CTE on this issue was satisfactory.

Looking back on the first two years of activity of the CTE, what conclusions can be drawn? Despite our active role and our ambitions, the substantive results we sought have been shown to be at present unachievable. Does this mean that the process in Geneva has been a total failure? I think not, and the best way to substantiate this assessment is by resuming what the CTE did achieve. First, the extensive analytical work on MEAs, ecolabelling and trade liberalization has brought a much clearer understanding of the great complexities of the relationship between trade policy and environmental policy: in the trade community, in the environment community and in the development community. The value of this must not be underestimated. The first fruit of this understanding is better policy coordination in many national administrations in these different areas, both in the development of MEAs, and in domestic legislation – a small step forward if you like, but not an insignificant one, and one that may well decrease the chance of damaging and unnecessary conflicts. In the international community the importance of meeting development concerns is better understood. The fear among many developing countries, to which I referred earlier, that environmental protection could lead to new forms of 'green' protectionism has been taken seriously. In short, the conclusions, although unquestionably disappointing, do provide some useful foundations on which to take build up the work in this area.

How, then, should work on trade and environment continue after Singapore? I remain firmly convinced that the WTO needs the so-called 'green window' and we will continue to seek this result in the future. The European Union should therefore not give up any of its ambitions in future WTO debates. For the reasons that I have set out earlier, the WTO has to be provided with instruments that allow it to balance the sometimes conflicting interests of further trade liberalization and environmental protection. At least it is now recognized that these issues need to be addressed at the multilateral level in order to meet the challenges of globalization and to channel this inevitable development in an orderly fashion. I think that a 'green window' is important if not crucial for the WTO's credibility as an organization that can seriously deal with today's challenges. How can we expect citizens, whether they are consumers, business people or environmental activists, to put trust in the multilateral trading system if it is seen as turning a blind eye to the environment?

Concrete work on trade and environment in the CTE will resume soon and the EU will remain actively involved in its work. We will certainly continue our efforts to obtain concrete results. The obstacles that we have encountered in the first two years of the CTE's existence, however, require a revision *not* of our ambitions, but of the timing. Even with more support from the United States or Canada or from other OECD countries, it is not likely that developing countries will radically change their attitudes. We should therefore face up to reality, and accept that it will be very difficult to reach consensus on the major questions before the next WTO Ministerial Meeting in 1998.

In those circumstances, it would not be sensible to put emphasis on the need for quick results. The forthcoming CTE meetings are probably best used for a further deepening of the analytical work that has taken place over the last two years. In certain respects, time is running in favour of the EU's general approach, since recent jurisprudence of the WTO Appellate Body in the Gasoline case seems to indicate a move towards the establishment of a more flexible doctrine on measures taken under Article XX of the GATT for reasons of environmental protection.

Some issues already on the agenda could be further developed. The trade-related aspects of the Climate Change Convention, for example, merit the particular attention of the CTE. Since this is a more technical subject than, for example, MEAs and ecolabelling, I see some true scope for concrete progress. A closer look at the energy sector and its implications for the environment would also be a useful exercise.

My answer to the question in the title of your conference – 'Trade and Environment: Conflict or Compatibility?' – is a clear one. The two *are* compatible, and should be mutually supportive. An open world trading system is not inimical to the achievement of environmental objectives. We have yet to achieve rules to establish the relationship between the two. The task of achieving such rules is taking longer than we would like, but we shall not give up the struggle.

Chapter 2

Trade Versus Environment: The Evidence

2.1 Introduction
Frits Schlingemann

The trade community is concerned about the abuse of environmental measures, particularly unilateral measures, for protectionist purposes. It is also worried about the increasing use of the trade regime to achieve environmental goals. Environmental protection should not be pursued at the cost of free trade. A main reason is that trade liberalization promotes development, and a lack of development will lead to further environmental decline. Sound environmental policies, capacity building and technology transfer – 'positive measures', as we call it in the trade and environment jargon – should be the subjects and names of the environmental game.

It is understandable that the trade community is concerned. Trade liberalization can indeed be an engine for development. Increased market access is an essential element in the pursuit of traditional economic growth. But the protection of nature and natural resources is also essential for development, and in many countries is certainly a requirement for sustained longer-term economic growth. What is more, environmental damage is often irreversible. And as UNEP's recently published *Global Environmental Outlook* reveals, we have overstretched the tolerance and capacity of the physical environment to allow for unconditioned economic growth and are close to threatening the very limits of life on earth.

We all – the trade community and the environmental community alike – share the responsibility for safeguarding and maintaining life on earth. Environmental degradation with irreversible impact is gaining pace on us, and policy-makers and legislators have to act collectively and urgently to reverse this trend. Considering that so-called positive measures often suffer from long incubation periods or yield only partial results, the use of trade measures for achieving environmental goals will have to form part of their decision-making tools.

We from the environment community therefore claim that the trade community must collaborate with us. The trade community, as we witnessed in Singapore, is not yet fully convinced. It has started to accept the suggestion, however, that trade liberalization and environmental protection are no more inherently supportive than they are inherently antithetical. We may well, and indeed should continue to, identify opportunities for mutual benefit and exploit those to the full. This will help build mutual understanding, and in the final instance consensus, between the two groups on the path to follow towards real sustainable development. We will not escape, however, the need to set the priorities right and take decisions on matters that divide the two communities. Preventing irreversible damage to the environment is an issue that can never be compromised.

2.2 Trade-related environmental impacts: how much is a dolphin worth?
James Lee

This paper looks at nine multilateral cases in order to determine relative trade-offs between trade costs and environmental benefits. These trade-offs are useful to policy-makers and the public in ascertaining the value in such measures.

Whereas one can collect trade data that are comparable, at least in economic terms, this is not possible with environmental data. There is little inter-comparability between the environmental cases; they involve differing species and habitats and differing ways of determining worth. Thus, there may be more compatibility *within* each case than *across* them.

The cases and concepts in this research are part of the Trade Environment Database (TED), created by myself at the School of International Service, Washington, DC. TED is a collection of over 400 case studies on trade and environment that are organized around 28 attributes, such as the environmental problem, the relevant legal measure, and the type of habitat.[17] For each case, relevant trade categories are identified using the

Standard International Trade Classification (SITC), revision 3. With the proper SITC categories, it is possible to run data searches for the period under which these measures were in place. These data searches were carried out using UN Conference on Trade and Development (UNCTAD) software called *GREENTRADE*.[18]

Case A: US–Japan apple

Japan officially opened its markets to apple imports in 1971. Because of phytosanitary import standards, however, no American apples entered Japan for 22 years. As growers sought to meet each obstacle of regulation (including fire blight and coddling moths), the Japanese allegedly erected new hurdles. Finally, in 1993, American growers filed a formal complaint with the US Trade Representative (USTR). The US Secretary of Agriculture and the USTR sent a letter to Japan's Minister of Agriculture, who, in return, promised to open Japan's markets to American apples in 1994. The USTR also threatened Japan with Congressional retaliation under Section 301 of American trade law.

In 1995, Japanese import standards allowed the import of American apples, which sold for less than half the price of Japanese apples. Longer-term estimates of US apple exports to Japan were quite optimistic. The USTR predicted that three to four years after the Japanese lifted trade barriers American apple exporters to Japan could generate sales of approximately $75 million per year. Ironically, after a quick start, American apple sales fell far short of that total; Japanese consumers found American apples too sour and too disfigured.

---

[17] The TED case studies are available on the World Wide Web at: http://gurukul.ucc. american.edu/ted/ted.htm

[18] All dollar figures given in this section refer to US$ except where otherwise noted.

Trade impacts

Between 1971 and 1993, Japan imported only 4,500 boxes of apples, all from South and North Korea. In June 1993, Japan allowed the importation of 235 tons of apples from New Zealand. 'But due to high quarantine costs, the price of the New Zealand apples was nearly twice that of Fuji [Japanese] apples.'[19] In 1995, Japan's apple imports rose from virtually nothing to $6.7 million. American apple exports totalled $6.0 million, or 87% of the Japanese import total, followed by New Zealand ($0.5 million), and Turkey and South Korea ($0.1 million each). The Daiei supermarket chain began sales of American apples, pricing them 20%–30% lower than domestic apples. The most popular home-grown Fuji apples were priced between 80 yen (80 cents) and 150 yen ($1.50) each.[20]

How do Japan's apple imports compare with those of other East Asian countries? In 1995, Taiwan and Hong Kong imported about 4 million 42-pound boxes of Washington apples. In January 1995, Japan imported 400,000 boxes. By the end of March, only 100,000 more boxes had been sold and American growers stopped shipping any more. In retrospect, American sales by 31 March 1995 were much less than originally projected as a result of more open Japanese markets.[21]

American apple export performance in Japan stands in stark contrast to the profile of American apple exports to all of East Asia. Japanese imports of American apples actually accounted for only 4% of total East Asian apple consumption. Hong Kong, whose population is about 5% of Japan's and per capita income is lower, accounted for 28.1% of total East Asian apple imports from the United States. Thailand followed with 15.4% and Indonesia with 8.9%. Even Singapore's imports were about double the size of Japan's in this period.

---

[19] David Holley, 'No More Forbidden Fruit: US Apples Make a Crunchy Debut after Japan Lifts Ban', *Los Angeles Times* (16 January 1995), p. D1.

[20] Reuters Limited, 'US Trade Demands Bear Fruit in Japan', European Community Report (7 January 1995), Saturday, BC cycle, Tokyo.

[21] Marvin Dreyer, 'US Apples Try Another Slice of Japan', *Los Angeles Times* (home ed), (18 December 1995), p. D4, from the Electric Library on the Web. Washington state accounts for 90% of US apple production, producing 100 m boxes per year.

Environmental impacts

Prevention of species introduction via trade, and the possible destruction of Japanese apple groves, provide the basis of the case and the justification for phytosanitary regulations. Foreign organisms have traditionally wreaked havoc on many of the world's forests. The Nematode case (Case D below) illustrates the significant economic and trade costs arising from such a wood infestation. The environmental benefits in the case are perhaps best measured by the total Japanese apple consumption of 52 million boxes, in so far as nearly all of that comes from Japanese producers. If an infestation were to occur, this might well be the maximum level of annual loss. Perhaps half a million dollars' worth of American apples entered Japan that year or about 1% of the total, a small amount in terms of trade coverage.

Case B: GATT tuna-dolphin

In August 1990 the United States banned imports of Mexican tuna because Mexico had not taken steps to reduce the number of eastern tropical Pacific dolphins killed through tuna fishing. In January 1991 Mexico appealed the case to a GATT dispute settlement panel. The panel eventually ruled in favour of Mexico. The ruling was due in part to the discriminatory manner in which the United States implemented the measure and in part to the GATT resistance to cases where the process of production is a major factor. After great success in reducing dolphin deaths, 1997 US legislation put into place measures that made compliance easier and less costly.

Trade impacts

Mexico's exports of tuna to the United States fell from $13 million in 1989 to $3.2 million in 1990 in anticipation of the ban. Trade bottomed out at $1.2 million in 1991 and gradually rose to $4.0 million in 1994. Presumably, this rise indicates an increase in the fleet that recapitalized to meet dolphin-safe requirements. However, some believe that Mexico is importing tuna from Asian countries not covered by the ban and shipping it on to the United States.

France followed Mexico's GATT complaint with one of its own against the United States. France's imports of unprepared or raw tuna from Mexico were $5.1 million in 1989 (none recorded for the 1991–4 period). The American action also applied to French prepared tuna exports. American imports of canned tuna from France fell from $8.1 million to zero for the 1990–4 period. Mexico and the European Union maintain that they have also lost trade because of US tuna restrictions on Mexico and other countries. The EU asserts that its tuna exports to the United States fell by 4 million ECU per year.[22]

Environmental impacts

The US Commerce Department estimated that dolphin kill rates for vessels from Mexico, Venezuela, Vanuatu, Spain and the Cayman Islands, Costa Rica, El Salvador and Panama were two to four times higher (100,000 per year in total) than American kill rates.[23] Mexico alone killed an estimated 50,000 dolphins every year.[24]

Progress in decreasing tuna-fishing-related dolphin deaths has been substantial. 'Figures compiled by the Inter-American Tropical Tuna Commission show that dolphin deaths associated with tuna fishing in the eastern tropical Pacific have fallen from 133,000 in 1986 to 3,600 in 1993'.[25] Over 99% of dolphins trapped by nets were released unharmed. Dolphin populations can withstand an annual harvest of 1 in 200 animals. Recent mortality rates for dolphins are well below that threshold: last year it was approximately 1 in 2,700 dolphins. In fact, dolphins are not the only animals threatened by tuna fishing. 'A typical catch from 1,000 tons of

---

[22] 'European Boycott Urged on Mexican Tuna', *LDC Debt Report/Latin America Markets*, 4/21 (10 June 1991), p. 9.

[23] 'Panel Ruling on Dolphin Protection and the Environment', before the Subcommittee on Health and the Environment of the House Energy and Commerce Committee, 27 September 1991, p. 2.

[24] Stuart Auerbach, 'Raising a Roar over a Ruling', *Washington Post* (1 October 1991), p. D6.

[25] Frances Williams, 'GATT Shuts Door on Environmentalists', *Financial Times* (21 July 1994), p. 6. Also see Warren Christopher, 'Fact Sheet: Mexico's Marine Conservation Efforts', *Dispatch* (1 May 1994), p. 19.

tuna includes two sharks, 29 dolphins, five billfish and an average of less than one sea turtle, according to tuna commission data.'[26]

Case C: US–Canada lobster

Is the *Homarus Americanus* (American Lobster) in danger of extinction? This question was central to the US–Canada lobster dispute which began in 1992. American customs officials rejected Canadian lobster imports because they were small in size and therefore deemed immature specimens that were protected under US law. Canada countered that these lobsters were mature, but were simply smaller because of the colder waters in Canada. A binational panel determined that the lobsters were in danger of extinction and management restrictions were legitimately placed on lobster fishing. More specifically, the case focused on the administrative problems in distinguishing legal from illegal lobsters. Here, the panel sided with the United States on the grounds of administrative expense.

Trade impacts

Canada's lobster exports to the United States were $95.4 million in 1988. Exports fell to a low of $35.4 million in 1991 and rose to $120.6 million in 1994. Arguably, some of the decline may have been attributable to the weak American economy in 1991.

In the lobster dispute, Canada claimed potential losses of about $42.3 million per year. The United States claimed that a more realistic figure would lie between C$11.1 million and C$23.7 million (US$10 to US$21 million) annually. The United States claimed that the Canadian trade estimate was too high because small lobsters would continue to be harvested, and also that these measures would lead not to losses but to conservation for later sales: in ten years, the United States argued, Canada could see benefits equal to $C4.7 million (US$4.2 million) annually through stock replenishments.

---

[26] Betsy Carpenter, 'What Price Dolphin?', *US News & World Report*, 116/23 (13 June 1994), p. 71.

In 1988, the American lobster catch (14,462 tons) was valued at $95.4 million. Most lobsters are consumed domestically, with only 2,500 tons per year ($23.5 million) being exported. Imports account for 45%–50% of the total lobster consumption in the United States. Canada's lobster catch in 1988 was 40,392 tons. Canada sold 48% (19,619 tons) live, of which 14,528 tons were exported to the United States – a total value of C$192 million (about US$172.8 million). Furthermore, of 80 million pounds of lobster harvested in Canada in 1998, 56 million were exported to the United States live, canned or frozen.

Both Canada and the United States agree that the total Canadian lobster landings falling below the US federal minimum lobster size requirements were 8–8.4% in 1990, 12.1–12.4% in 1991, and 16.1–16.9% in 1992. Canada asserted that legal harvests from Canadian waters that did not meet the US federal minimum size requirement and were exported to the United States were actually much higher: 18% in 1990, 26% in 1991 and 34% in 1992.

Environmental impacts

This case represents a conflict between two reasonable positions. Lobster stocks are low and need management. The problem is that systems for administrative import calibration are not sufficient for differentiating between those sub-species in need of protection and those that are not. What is required is a synchronous system. Conserving the supply and diversity of lobster is necessary, but the irony is that the two systems came into conflict in areas where there are clearly overlapping interests. The environmental value in this case pertains to Canadian lobsters. A collapse of lobster stocks would cost Canada $360 million per year. The price of lobster protection is roughly their wholesale price: $5.95 per pound. (This problem may occur indirectly. Octopi prey on lobsters, and increases in their numbers may pose a threat to lobster stocks. The major predator of the octopus is the shark, and shark populations are in decline worldwide. Thus, shark over-fishing may pose a threat to lobster populations.)

Case D: Canada–EC nematode

In 1990, the EC banned the import of untreated, green (or raw) softwood lumber. The ban was a means to avoid the inadvertent importation of the pinewood nematode into Europe, which could have destructive effects on the local forest environment.[27] Until recently, both the United States and Canada possessed a derogation to this ban, allowing the export of Canadian and American softwood to continue provided that special certifications of inspection and debarking standards were met. This derogation was scheduled to end on 1 October 1993. The EC then imposed the ban, particularly affecting Canada's wood exports.

Trade impacts

Canadian wood exports to EC countries covered by the nematode ban peaked at $945.9 million in 1991 (a jump from $709.6 million in 1990) and fell to $315.3 million in 1993; in 1994, they rose slightly to $323 million. Most of the decline was the result of the ban, and in particular was due to a drop in sales to the United Kingdom. From a peak of $495.4 million in 1990, Canadian sales to the UK fell by about one-third in the following year and declined to $153.2 million in 1994, a drop of over two-thirds from its peak.

Wood exports from the United States to the EC fell by much less. American exports rose from $253.1 million in 1988 to $323.6 million in 1991, and declined by about one-third to $204.3 million in 1994. American exports to the UK were about the same in 1990 and 1994. The US experienced export declines in Germany, where exports fell from $33.9 million in 1991 to zero in the 1992–4 period. Italy showed contrary patterns: American exports rose from $95.5 million in 1988 to $130.3 million in 1991, before falling back to $61.9 million in 1994. Canadian exports to Italy actually increased twofold over the 1988–94 period, from $30.9 million in 1988 to $69.5 million in 1994.

In addition to trade losses, new capital equipment to meet the import

---

[27] 'British Columbia Softwood Lumber Industry Explores New Method to Fight EC Export Ban', *International Trade Reporter* (BNA) (1 September 1993).

requirements was needed, adding to the overall economic cost of the measure. Canada estimated that purchasing the kiln facilities would initially cost $500,000 and add approximately $72 million to the annual production costs of lumber mills.[28] Another way to look at the economic impact is through prices. The price effect, based on the adoption of the proposed Canadian heat method (the cheapest alternative because it is more time- and cost-effective), increases production costs by 8–15%. In comparison, the EC kiln-drying method could increase costs from anywhere between 16% and 40%.

Environmental impacts

'The pinewood nematode, *bursaphelencus xylophilus*, is native to North America. It eats wood and is carried from tree to tree by bark beetles of the genus *Monocamus*. In North America, the nematode does not cause disease. But when the worm was introduced to Japan in wood from the US during the 1980s, it caused a disease called pine wilt which killed many trees.'[29] In 1991, inspectors at the French port of Le Havre found worm-holes in a shipment of Canadian timber that was supposed to have been kiln-dried, a process that should kill all nematodes. One Canadian official said that the bugs actually came from American wood.[30]

No one can deny the economic value of forests to European countries. Finland and Sweden run wood trade surpluses of billions of dollars each year. Finland's wood exports make up about a third of its total exports, and Sweden's about a sixth. The UK, however, has the largest wood trade deficit in Europe: again, several billion dollars per year. Sweden's per ton production costs were about four times as great as Canada's and Finland's.[31] The economics may well be in saving jobs more than forests.

---

[28] Peter Kennedy, 'Atlantic Mills', *Financial Post* (17 July 1993), p. 6.

[29] Debora MacKenzie, 'Timber Pest Prompts Import Curb; Pine Nematode Bursaphelencus xylophilus in Canadian Timber', *New Scientist*, 138/1874 (22 May 1993), p. 7.

[30] Bernard Simon, 'Canada Accuses EC over Lumber Ban', *Financial Times* (13 July 1993), Commodities and Agriculture, p. 26.

[31] Andrew J. Ewing and Raymond Chalk, *The Forest Industries Sector: An Operational Strategy for Developing Countries*, World Bank Technical Paper no. 83 (Washington, DC: World Bank, 1988).

Case E: Ontario beer taxes

After several years of negotiations and two GATT panel decisions against
Canada, in April 1992 the United States and Canada finally reached
agreement over Canadian policies *vis-à-vis* American imported beer. Five
days later, the Ontario government placed an 'environmental tax' of $0.10
per can on aluminium beer containers, in order to encourage the use of
recyclable glass containers. In addition to the environmental tax, the
Ontario liquor board imposed a $2.53 per case warehouse charge on
foreign beers, mostly American. The United States claimed this tax was
merely economic protection, because it did not apply to any other
aluminium beverage containers except beer, and canning would naturally
be the choice of foreign beer exporters. The United States then responded
by placing a tax of $3 per case (50% *ad valorem*) on beer imported from
Ontario. The Ontario provincial government retaliated with an additional
tax of $3 per case on American beer. Although Ontario offered to settle the
dispute through the GATT, the United States refused.

Trade impacts

Beer trade between Canada and the United States shows two distinct
patterns. American beer exports show clear cyclical patterns over the
1980–94 period. These cycles have a duration of about five years. Peaks in
American exports to Canada came in 1980, 1985, 1989 and 1994 and
immediately dropped in the years thereafter. For the 1980–94 period,
American exports rose about 30% in non-adjusted data. The range of
exports was from $6.2 million in 1984 to $34.3 million in 1989. With
respect to the current case, American exports dropped from $26.9 million
in 1991 to $20.7 million the following year and to $12.9 million in 1993.

Canadian beer exports to the United States show no cyclical pattern. To
the contrary, Canada's exports show a consistent and continued rise over
the period with relatively few drops from prior-year totals. For the 1980–
94 period, Canada's exports rose from $90.1 million to $197.8 million,
easily doubling in value. During the period of dispute, Canada's exports
surged by about one-third.

The leading American exporters are Stroh Breweries and Heileman Breweries, and the leading Canadian exporters are Molson Breweries and Labatt's Breweries. However, some believe domestic market sales may be larger than trade sales.[32] The United States imposed an *ad valorem* tariff of 50% on beer imports from Ontario province only. Therefore, prices for American beer differed markedly from province to province in Canada.

Environmental impacts

One can compare two similar recycling procedures implemented by the Blitz-Weinhard Brewing Company, located in Portland, and the Rainier Brewing Company, located in Seattle. The Blitz-Weinhard Brewing Company has reused 28 million bottles, saving enough landfill space to fill Portland's Memorial Coliseum 20 feet deep and enough energy to serve 2,007 homes a year. The Rainier Brewing company has refilled 20 million bottles, which equals 16,000 cubic yards of landfill space and power used annually by 1,434 homes. If the 16,000 cubic yards of bottles saved by Rainier are added to Blitz-Weinhard's 22,440 cubic yards, Memorial Coliseum would be filled to a depth of 35 feet. In addition, the inspection, sterilization and refilling procedures save 84% of the energy required to make new bottles.[33]

Case F: US–Venezuela gasoline

The Clean Air Act Amendments of 1990 (P.L. 101–549) required the use of reformulated gasoline (RFG) that met standards set under the US Environmental Protection Agency's Clean Air Act (CAA), starting on 1 January 1995. The Environmental Protection Agency (EPA) published new standards, requiring foreign refiners to increase the oxygen content and reduce the aromatic level in order to achieve cleaner RFG: the

---

[32] Leo Ryan, 'Ontario's Can Tax Angers Aluminum, Beer Industries', *Journal of Commerce* (16 May 1992).

[33] Consider these values in terms of the tipping fees per ton at sanitary landfills, where municipal solid waste is disposed. In Indiana, the tipping fee was about $27 per ton (Solid Waste Price Index, *Solid Waste Digest*, Chartwell Information Publishers, Alexandria, Va).

acceptable RFG standards are 2% oxygen, no lead or other heavy metals, and 1% benzene. In addition, RFG is also subject to performance standard tests that prescribe a 15% improvement in air quality in 1995, and a 25% improvement by 2000.

Venezuela and Brazil complained to the WTO that such baselines were discriminatory to foreign producers. In early 1996, the WTO determined that the law did discriminate against Venezuela and Brazil. The United States appealed and lost the case.

Trade impacts

The total value of Venezuela's gasoline exports to the United States declined in the 1990s. Having risen from $721.3 million in 1989 to $821.2 million in 1990, they collapsed to $440 million in 1991, and the following year rose to $503.9 million. After this brief upsurge, imports continued to fall, to $214.2 million in 1994. Petroleos de Venezuela SA is investing $1 billion in its refineries to produce reformulated gasoline that will conform to the American demands. Also, it will spend $500 million on refineries to control atmospheric pollutants, treat liquid effluent and dispose of solid wastes. As a result, the Venezuelan protection price for one gallon of gasoline ($0.73) could be about twice the price of American domestic refiners'.

Environmental impacts

The disputed measure was intended to protect air quality in the United States, especially in northeast and midwestern urban areas. The measure was expected to produce a marginal improvement in air quality. The American law that was challenged included benefits to methane producers, mostly to corn growers located in the Midwest. Although methane energy is cleaner than gasoline in cars, the energy costs when considered with its agricultural production and conversion costs make it less cost-effective. Thus, the overall environmental benefits of the measure are less clear, considering energy-conversion and land-use costs. In general, gas is much less carbon-intensive than other existing energy sources such as oil and coal.

One study concluded that every ton of sulphur dioxide emitted into the air causes more than $3,000 of health-related damage per person in affected communities. When multiplied by the tons of pollutants emitted and the number of affected communities, the resulting cost is $25 billion per year from the effects of midwestern coal-fired power plants alone.[34] Ozone, another of the components of air pollution, is responsible for at least 90% of pollution-related crop damage in the United States. The National Acid Precipitation Assessment Program concluded in its 1987 report that current levels of ozone were reducing cotton and soybean crop yields by approximately 7% and reducing alfalfa yields by more than 30%. It estimated crop losses at between 5% and 10% of total production, representing economic losses of $5.4 billion.

Case G: US sanctions on Taiwan

The population of the world's mega-fauna – such as rhinoceros and tiger – is in rapid decline. The world's rhinoceros population fell 90% in the last 23 years, to a total of less than 10,000 animals worldwide, and the tiger population fell 95% to 5,000 animals. The rhinoceros is among the world's most endangered mammals, and one of the first species to be covered by the 1973 Convention on International Trade in Endangered Species. Many countries have violated the CITES ban on trade in endangered species, and in a unilateral act, the United States targeted Taiwan. In March 1994 it placed retaliatory sanctions on that country for its continued trade in rhinoceros and tiger products, and then rescinded them about a year later.

Trade impacts

American sanctions on Taiwan for trade in CITES-related products equalled about $25 million, covering coral, mollusc shell jewellery, lizard, snake, and crocodile skin shoes, and other leather products.[35] A similar

---

[34] David B. Webster, 'The Free Market for Clean Air', *Business and Society Review* (Summer 1994), pp. 34–5.

[35] 'US Puts Sanctions on Taiwan', *New York Times* (12 April 1994), p. D1.

import ban would cost China between $50 and $60 million a year.[36]

Taiwan was a major importer of rhinoceros horn for the period 1979–85. Supplies came mainly from South Africa, Hong Kong and Singapore. Taiwan is not a member of CITES because it is not recognized by the United Nations. Nevertheless, the government banned trade in rhino horn in 1985, at least in law; trade continued, however, at least until 1989. Taiwan is believed to be stocking horn and acting as an entrepôt, since Macao and Singapore imposed successful bans on the trade in 1985 and 1986. The Taiwan government also undertook a mandatory registration programme, completed in 1990, that showed a stock of 1,456 kg for 410 registrants. However, surveys in 1991 showed that approximately 1,800 pharmacies stocked horn, and suggested stockpiles of at least 3,712 kg and possibly as much as 8,943 kg.[37]

The rhino horn trade may be worth as much as $3 million annually.[38] Based on an average horn weight of 3.5 pounds, an African rhino horn is worth around $1,500, about $430 per pound. Between 1982 and 1986, China imported 10,621 kg of African horn, worth about $2.3 million, and 433 kg of Asian horn, which is much more expensive per pound than its African counterpart. Though not declared, the origins of these imports were believed to be North Yemen, Hong Kong, Macao, Taiwan, Singapore and Thailand. Mandatory registration of stocks in 1988 revealed 9,874 kg in various medicine corporations, excluding stocks in retail medicine, museums and private ownership.

Environmental impacts

The sanctions were meant to preserve remaining stocks of tiger and rhinoceros in the wild. These two species have been decimated over the last decade, with at least 90% of their populations killed. Why preserve them? The moral argument is that we have an obligation to preserve such major species. The economic argument is that, through tourism and other

[36] According to Genette Hemley of TRAFFIC.
[37] N. Leader-Williams, *The World Trade in Rhino Horn: A Review* (Washington, DC: Traffic International, 1992), p. 22.
[38] Joanne Burgess, *The Environmental Effects of Trade* (Paris: OECD, 1994), p. 133.

activities, species protection is affordable.

In the 1970s, about one-half of rhino horn exports went to Yemen and the other half to East Asia. In Yemen and Oman, rhino horn is used to make the handle and sheath of the traditional dagger, or jambiyya. Male Yemenis and Omanis have worn these rhino daggers for centuries and they constitute part of the rite of male initiation. Substitutes, such as antelope horn, are now used. However, these substitutes have been less acceptable in East Asia, where the horn is in demand as an aphrodisiac.

Case H: Shrimp and sea turtle

The Earth Island Institute, a San Francisco-based environmental organization, filed a suit on 24 February 1992 to protect sea turtles, forcing the US Departments of State and Commerce to comply with the federal law banning shrimp imports from countries that endanger sea turtles when they trawl for shrimp. The law was applied to countries with shrimp operations in the Caribbean and the western central Atlantic. The Earth Island Institute believed that the law should also extend to include Pacific and Indian Ocean nations such as Japan, Thailand, Indonesia, India, Malaysia and South Korea, as well as Mexico and Brazil. Countries currently operating under the law account for only 10% of the world's annual shrimp harvest. Mexico adopted the regulation but only Surinam's shrimp were actually banned when the law went into effect. However, a new round of shrimp import bans began in May 1996 and were the subject of appeal to the WTO in 1997 by several Asian countries (see Section 4.3).

Trade impacts

Turtle protection regulations were put in place on 1 May 1991. In 1989, American shrimp exports from Mexico were $281.3 million. In anticipation of the ban, Mexican exports fell to $176.5 million in 1990 before recovering again in 1991. By 1994, Mexican imports had risen to nearly to the 1989 total, at $256.5 million. Although Mexico was the largest shrimp exporter, relative impacts on other countries were much greater.

Venezuela's exports fell over 50% between 1989 and 1990, from $47.1 million to $22.6 million, and Brazil's fell by about the same amount from their 1989 value of $44.6 million. Costa Rica's imports dropped from $11.3 million to $3.7 million, or by about two-thirds. Panama's imports dropped from $69 million to $41.8 million.

The top shrimp exporters to the United States are India, Indonesia, Thailand, Mexico, Malaysia, Korea and Japan. The measure 'could effect shrimp imports from more than 80 nations totalling as much as $1.8 billion – more than 75% [by value] of all shrimp consumed in this country'.[39] In 1988, 331 million pounds of shrimp worth $506 million were imported to the United States. More than 30,000 US commercial fishermen and their families rely on shrimp for jobs and many times that number work in shore-side processing plants.[40]

Turtle-excluder devices (TEDs) have been developed for shrimp and fish trawls to reduce incidental deaths. TEDs are panels of large mesh webbing, or metal grids, inserted into the funnel-shaped shrimp nets. As the nets are dragged along the bottom, shrimp and other small animals pass through the TED and into the 'cod end' of the net, the narrow bag at the end of the funnel where the catch is collected. Sea turtles, sharks and fish too large to get through the panel are deflected out through an escape hatch.[41] TEDs enable turtles to escape the trawl net and prevent them from drowning, reducing the number of turtles killed by shrimp trawls by at least 97%.

An official with the Texas Shrimp Association, Wilma Anderson, said the US regulations requiring use of TEDs would cost the Association's 700 members 'additional gear expense and additional production loss'. She said compliance with new rules requiring TEDs had cost shrimpers between $30,000 and $35,000 per boat per year. Fishermen, who believe that the TED causes their nets to dump 20% or more of the shrimp as well, call them 'trawler eliminator devices'. One source notes a 6% loss of shrimp harvest resulting from the requirement to use TEDs. The law

---

[39] *Christian Science Monitor* (14 May 1992).
[40] Jack Rudloe and Anne Rudloe, 'Shrimpers and Lawmakers Collide over how to Save the Sea Turtles', *Smithsonian* 20 (December 1989), pp. 44–55.
[41] Sara Strong, 'Battle to Save Sea Turtles Cooling', *Christian Science Monitor* 18 (October 1989), p. 8.

required foreign shrimpers in the targeted nations to use TEDs, and thus to incur similar additional gear expenses and production losses.

Environmental impacts

It is estimated that American shrimp trawls drown 11,179 sea turtles annually, a figure recently updated by the National Academy of Sciences to 55,000.[42] According to National Marine Fishing Service (NMFS) estimates, approximately 48,000 sea turtles are caught each year on shrimp trawlers in the southeastern United States and approximately 11,000 die. Of those, 10,000 are loggerheads and 750 are Kemp's Ridleys.[43]

The requirement to use TEDs saves about 150,000 turtles per year. Most sea turtle species are in fact endangered. The turtles are used for meat and leather and the shells for ornament. In a related case on the hawksbill turtle, the United States threatened to impose sanctions on Japan for continued imports of the hawksbill turtle shell, in the form of either a ban or high duties on imports of Japan's wildlife products, such as pearls and ornamental carp, which constitute a $200 million dollar market.[44]

Case I: US ban on driftnets

In the early 1980s, Japanese fleets (as well as Taiwanese and South Korean) began to use large-scale driftnets in the North Pacific Ocean to catch salmon, tuna, squid and other species. A driftnet typically stretches as wide as 40 miles and traps many species. Among its unintended victims are marine mammals such as whales, dolphins, porpoises, fur seals and other sea animals including sea turtles and even sea birds.

Driftnet fishing is believed to have contributed to a decrease in the population of such economically valuable fish as tuna, marlin, swordfish and salmon in the North Pacific Ocean. The United States, Canada and Russia were concerned about the rapid destruction of valuable sea

---

[42] *Audubon* (September 1995).
[43] Rudloe and Rudloe, 'Shrimpers and Lawmakers Collide', p. 44.
[41] Makiko Shinohara, 'Japan and US at Loggerheads over Endangered Sea Turtles', *Christian Science Monitor* (10 May 1991), p. 7.

resources and restricted their fishing, especially driftnets, in the North
Pacific region. The UN General Assembly adopted a series of resolutions
calling for a moratorium on driftnet fishing on the high seas by 30 June
1992, later put back to December 1992.[45] As a result, Japan halted driftnet
fishing on the high seas and the United States banned the import of
products caught in driftnets.

Trade impacts

Driftnets have been commonly used by many countries in coastal waters.
However, Japanese driftnet fishing began to attract attention in the mid-
1980s when Japan and other Asian countries began to send large fleets to
the North Pacific Ocean to catch especially tuna and squid. Those fishing
boats were blamed not only for the indiscriminate destruction of marine
life but also for the poaching of North Pacific salmon. Japan operated
about 900 driftnet vessels and earned $300 million a year from them.

Few products from driftnet catches are thought to have been exported to
the United States or any other country because they are consumed in
Japanese (and other) domestic markets. Since trade data do not record
catches by method used, little substantial information on the trade impact
from the driftnet ban exists. Sanctions on driftnet fishing were substantial
across a number of dimensions. HR-2152 and its companion bill, S-884,
allow the government to revoke or suspend fishing and processing permits
to fishermen who violate the law, and to increase fines from $25,000 to
$100,000. The reauthorization bill set a spending ceiling of $75 million
for monitoring programmes under the act during the initial fiscal year, and
rose by $1 million a year through fiscal 1993. Perhaps 15,000 Japanese
fishermen who fish for red cuttlefish and albacore would be affected by
the measure.[46] South Korean driftnet fishermen caught 150,000 tons of

---

[45] *Expansion of the North Pacific High Seas Driftnet Fisheries: Hearing before a Subcommittee of the Committee on Appropriations, United States Senate* (Washington DC: US
Government Printing Office, 1990), p. 9; 'Gist: High-Seas Driftnet Fishing', US Department of State Dispatch (Washington DC: US Government Printing Office, 1992), p. 783.
[46] 'US Defers Sanctions on Taiwan, Korea Driftnet Fishing', Kyoto News Service, Japan
Economic Newswire (19 October 1991).

fish stocks in the past seven months, earning more than 200 billion won and sustaining the livelihood of more than 50,000 people.[47]

Environmental impacts

The biggest impact of driftnets is that they catch more than just their intended target. There are two categories of concern. The first issue is the high seas interception of salmon and steelhead trout of American and Canadian origin: under international law, the fish belong to the streams in which they originate. Second, there is concern over the incidental taking of other species of fish, marine mammals and seabirds (whales, dolphins and northern fur seals) that may have an aesthetic or commercial value. The Japanese squid industry in 1990 killed over 41 million non-target fish, sharks, sea birds, marine mammals and sea turtles.[48]

Millions of sea creatures were saved each year by the ban. Ranges for the destruction of wildlife and sea mammals from driftnets include: 75,000–875,000 seabirds, 20,000–200,000 metric tons of blue sharks, and marine mammals estimated in tens of thousands and upwards. Following the ban, there was a record coho salmon season in the United States. Prior to the ban, the average salmon catch in the North Pacific was 127 million tons; in 1993 the catch was 193 million, and in 1994 it was even higher.[49] Southeast Alaskan catches jumped over 100%, from 1.6 to 3.5 million.

Comparison of the cases

The most comparable impacts are for single species. It is possible to say with some degree of confidence, for example, that the adoption of TEDs saved the lives of many turtles; therefore, dollar values for saving the life of the animal can be calibrated. On this basis, the cost of saving the life is

---

[47] 'S. Korea to Try to Avert US Driftnet Sanctions', Reuters (23 October 1991).

[48] W. I. Bennet, 'Driftnet Fishing: US, Japan Agree on Moratorium', *Dispatch* 2 (2 December 1991), p. 875.

[49] Richard Bard, 'Record Coho Returns Point Finger at High Seas Squid Fleet By-catch', *National Fisherman* (1 February 1995), p. 15.

relatively modest. However, for the survival of the animal, these 'life savings' can mean two entirely different outcomes. For the sea turtle, it may be a further step away from extinction. For the dolphin, which is not endangered, it will have little effect on the survival of the species but everyone will probably sleep a lot better as a result.

The other benefits are not very comparable. For the apple and nematode cases, the value shown is an industry output figure. Table 2.1 shows the trade costs and environmental benefits and a 'score,' which represents the value for the benefit.

Table 2.1: Trade and environment scorecard

Case	Score	Trade cost ($m)	Environmental benefit
A: US–Japan apple	Prevention is 4% of total apple market	6.0	No infestation
B: GATT tuna-dolphin	$118 per dolphin	11.8	100,000 dolphins
C: US–Canada lobster	$7.90 per lobster	24.1	3.5 million lobsters
D: Canada–EC nematode	Prevention is 10% of wood import market	251.8	No infestation
E: US–Canada beer tax	$1,785 in landfill fees	14.0	Less landfill
F: US–Venezuela gasoline	Millions of dollars in health and agricultural costs	214.2	Better health and agricultural production
G: US sanctions on Taiwan	$1,673 per protecting existing animal	25.1	15,000 higher mammals exist
H: Shrimp and sea turtle	$699 per turtle	104.8	150,000 sea turtles
I: US ban on driftnets	$11.4 per other animal	40	3.5 million animals

The evaluation of the benefits to the environment in these cases is a difficult task. Whereas the trade data do provide a readily available basis for comparison, environmental benefits do not. This is because: (1) general knowledge on the subject is limited; and (2) no common system for comparison exists. None the less, there is some comparison for the cases between the trade costs and environmental benefits.

- In the apple case, trade costs were equal to $6.0 million per year, based on current American export totals. The regulation protected the $150 million Japanese apple industry. Therefore, the value of the measure can be considered in coverage terms. On this basis, the measure covers about 1% of the total Japanese apple market.
- The relative environmental value in the tuna-dolphin case is somewhat easier to compute. Trade costs were a maximum of $11.8 million per year to Mexico. In all, about 100,000 dolphins were alleged to have been saved per year. The value of each dolphin was therefore about $118.
- The lobster case cost about $24.1 million per year to Canada in trade. At an estimated import price, this is probably 5 million lobsters per year. Therefore, this is a fee of about $5 per lobster in order to sustain species stocks.
- The nematode case prevents infestation at a cost of perhaps $214.2 million per year. Europe's total wood imports are in the order of $25 billion per year to Canada. Therefore, the trade coverage ratio of the measure is about 10% of the total European impact market.
- In the beer taxes case, the actual cost in trade terms was $14 million per year, although this does not consider the American retaliation involved in the case. The actual landfill costs resulting from American beer exports are minimal. Based on landfill tipping fees for Indiana, which are about $25 per cubic ton, the actual costs are about $2,000 for disposing of, perhaps, 20 million beer bottles.
- The gasoline case is the most ambiguous in terms of measurement. The trade costs were $214 million but the benefits were much more general. There are clear benefits in better health and better agricultural production, but they are much more diffuse. Moreover, distinguishing the role of Venezuela from other air pollution factors is a major research problem.
- The Taiwan sanctions case was essentially a 'fine' of $25.1 million on Taiwan for trade in rhinoceros and tiger products. About 15,000 of these higher mammals exist, and therefore the fine for protecting future generations was about $1,673 per animal.

- The shrimp-turtle case is again easier to calculate because there are data on turtles. About 150,000 turtles were saved per year, equating to $699 per turtle.
- Trade data for the driftnet case do not exist. However, a shipment of 7.9 million squid is worth perhaps $40 million, and about 3.5 million other animals (birds, fish, etc.) are killed in the process. Saving these animals costs almost $12 each.

Conclusion

The question of the cost of trade measures designed to protect the environment is importantly one of timing. Measures that protect resources and cause short-term losses can later lead to recovery of resources and greater long-term trade. This is clear in species-specific cases (nematode, shrimp, lobster, Taiwan and driftnet). In the other cases, it is assumed that protecting the environment now is cheaper than protecting it later. The trade values noted here are static, rather then dynamic, representations.

The attempt here clearly shows that values inherent in environmental protection are difficult to calculate. If that task is daunting, ascribing the partial impacts of a measure within the context of value is even more troublesome. In addition, there is the chasm that exists between the differing types of environmental problem and the reasons for them. Given the milieu of differing calculations that need to be made, it is easy to see how this entire process could become very political.

It is assumed that efforts to protect the environment often create barriers to trade. This may be true in the short term, but not necessarily so in the long term. Over time, the impact of a measure may change in strength or even in direction. However, most efforts look primarily at short-term impacts. More work on long-term impacts and benefits needs to be undertaken.

The benefits in the cases are calculated on various bases. However, these comparisons lack true consistency. They do show some relative cost trade-offs that suggest that trade measures are good bargains for the environment the more they are focused on a species. It is enough to say more work is needed.

Discussion

Discussion following the presentation focused primarily on two topics. First, how accurate were the estimated costs? If a trade embargo imposed by one country simply led to diversion of exports to another, or into the domestic market, then the environmental problem might not have been alleviated at all. Dr Lee accepted that this was an important point, and one that needed further research. The environmental benefits of the measures in question could also be more precisely estimated; as in the driftnet case, they often went well beyond conservation of just one species.

The second main issue was the question of who actually bore the costs estimated in the various cases – the country implementing the measure (which might be expected to be prepared to pay the costs in exchange for the environmental benefits) or the exporters. In practice, it was generally the latter. Dr Lee argued for measures to be found that relieved developing-country exporters from the cost of trade measures and distributed them more widely – for example, to developed-country consumers through price premiums on environmentally benign products (such as 'dolphin-safe' labelled cans).

2.3 Competitiveness and investment[50]
Jonathan Barton

There is an assumption built into debates relating to environmental regulations and their impacts on firms. The assumption is that there is a global playing field and that movements of firms, investments and products will take place across this field as regulations create gradients by dint of their strengths and weaknesses in different states. The commonly held belief is that as regulations become more stringent there will be a

---

[50] This presentation was made as part of the EC-funded project: *Environmental Regulations, Globalization of Production and Technological Change*. This project is a three-year investigation into the environmental strategies of 'pollution-intensive' industries in the European Union as compared with their counterparts in the developing world and central and eastern Europe, and the implications of these strategies for production, trade and competitiveness. Other members of the research group are based at the Department of Human Geography, University of Oslo, and the Institute of New Technologies, United Nations University, Maastricht.

movement to sites of more relaxed controls. While this assumption might appear to be a logical one, based on firms making optimal and rational decisions, there is little evidence to support it. This is because firms are not necessarily economically rational, owing to the complex interplay of numerous interconnected factors relating to production and trade, and also because the simplicity of the notion of movement across the global playing field is not a realistic one.

The central questions to be addressed in terms of the environment and changes in trade and investment are as follows:

- Do different levels of environmental regulation between countries lead to industrial migration or affect investment flows in a 'race to the bottom'? and
- Can tougher environmental standards attract investment and affect, through trade, environmental regulations elsewhere?

Environmental regulations and regulatory compromise

The development of an international environmental agenda from a starting point in the early 1970s, principally from the Stockholm Conference in 1972, led to the emergence of controls and restrictions on levels of environmental contamination. For the first time, international business had to confront the fact that the environment would have to be regarded as an economic factor, alongside labour, transport and others, in considerations of production, trade and consumption. In this way, the environment became valued and recognized as a 'good', in terms of sustainability and future natural resource use, and as 'good economics', in that there was a recognition that the value of the environment would increase over time with resource depletion and public consciousness and pressure.

The integration of the environment into corporate strategy has been slow, since the regulations that were constructed at national and supranational levels were initially perceived as costs rather than benefits; the 'good economics' concept was slow to filter through to business. This perception was due partly to the fact that early regulations were motivated by ecological pressure groups and political responses. Business was slow to immerse itself in the construction of its own regulatory frameworks and to see them as being potentially useful tools for future competitiveness.

The positive elements of regulation, the benefits, have been recognized only slowly and have only recently been promoted strongly within academia. Naturally regulations lead (or at least should lead) to positive environmental outcomes, but the connection that business could also gain from these regulations and treat them as a long-term benefit rather than a long-term cost is a more recent development. It is Porter (author of *The Competitive Advantage of Nations*[51]) and van der Linde[52] who have put forward this positive, so-called 'win–win', argument most convincingly. They argue that regulations lead to innovation and adaptation in order to deal with the cost implications of the regulations. Managers become aware of the need to recognize efficiencies in production and sales, and they introduce more dynamic managerial practices and new technologies. While this may be costly in the initial stages, the argument is that these firms are well placed in the global market place as regulations become stricter elsewhere and firms are forced to follow suit. In this way, firms may become 'first movers' and enjoy the comparative advantages of having implemented environmental procedures and technologies at an early stage.

An example of this is the German 'pollution-intensive' industrial sectors, where strict early regulations relating to emissions levels gave rise to a flourishing environmental goods and services industry which currently accounts for the lion's share of the European market. While the 'pollution-intensive' industries were forced to invest in capital equipment and pass a keen eye over their process and production methods, these investments have put them in a strong position as similar regulatory frameworks have been adopted elsewhere and competitor firms have had to follow suit.

The counter-argument to Porter and van der Linde is offered by Palmer, Oates and Portney,[53] who suggest that innovation is not necessarily an

---

[51] M. Porter, *The Competitive Advantage of Nations* (London: Macmillan, 1990).

[52] M. Porter and C. van der Linde, 'Towards a New Conception of the Environment-Competitiveness Relationship', *Journal of Economic Perspectives*, 9:4 (1995), pp. 97–118.

[53] K. Palmer, W. E. Oates and P. R. Portney, 'Tightening Environmental Standards: The Benefit-Cost or the No-Cost Paradigm?', *Journal of Economic Perspectives*, 9:4 (1995), pp. 119–32.

outcome of tighter regulations since some firms may be unable to compete within the new framework. It is not logical, therefore, to state that innovation will be a response throughout the industrial sector under regulation. It is likely that some firms will innovate in response to regulation and others will lose competitiveness. Unlike Porter and van der Linde, the counter-argument assumes more of a zero-sum game within which not all firms can gain, but some will gain at others' expense.

Apart from these theoretical suppositions regarding firms' responses, research in the field reveals contradictory results based on different geographical areas and scales of survey. For this reason, regulations appear to have different impacts dependent on sector, region and specific firm circumstances. In this way, regulations are context-specific and need to be arrived at by a process of compromise with those agents involved in the regulatory procedure: the implementers, the monitors, the enforcers and those subject to the regulations. Without consensus and acceptance of what regulations seek to achieve and how these objectives can be realized, the regulations become costs rather than benefits. Without the recognition of 'good economics' and a starting point of the environmental 'good', business seeks ways of circumventing regulatory legislation to reduce the costs.

It is with this in mind that regulations should 'protect' those who pursue them without the threat of loss of market share or global competitiveness while longer-term environmental strategies are implemented. The relationship between the state regulatory authorities and the business community becomes an important one in this regard – both must feel that they are working towards long-term environmental goals which will feed back into successful business activities. To achieve longer-term security for firms engaged in environmental regulation implementation, there is a need for domestic governments to work within multilateral circles in order to create global support networks for firms involved in environmental restructuring. Only in this way can global flows of environmental 'goods' (green or eco-products) and 'bads' (pollution displacement) be addressed and promoted or curtailed. Sector-level and product-level research is required in order to establish how this can be effectively put into operation.

Competitiveness and environment

To assess the extent to which environmental regulations have impacted upon firm competitiveness requires an analysis of what constitutes competitiveness. It is the difficulty with the concept of competitiveness that makes comparison, especially at the global level, problematic. Having a simple notion of competitiveness, such as market share, may enable a firm to make assessments about its standing relative to competitors, but market share is dependent upon numerous interrelated factors that require deeper analysis. To separate out the factor of environmental regulations from these others is a complex process, and for this reason it is difficult to be sure to what extent it is environmental regulations that are affecting firm behaviour relative to other factors.

The European Union's *Competitiveness Database* provides a wide range of competitiveness indicators, within which environmental indicators are notably absent. The *Competitiveness Database* definition of competitiveness is: 'the ability of a firm, on a sustainable basis, to satisfy the needs of its customers more effectively than its competitors, by supplying goods and services more efficiently, in terms of price and non-price factors, than these competitors'.[54] Within such a broad working framework, the difficulties of separating out what does and does not constitute competitiveness, let alone targeting the influence of particular factors, become apparent.

Clearly, there will be a difference in competitiveness at various scales of analysis, from product through sector to national, regional (e.g. EU, NAFTA) and global levels. Regardless of these levels, the importance is to have a clear understanding of competitiveness for consistent comparison. Once this has been attained, the role of environmental regulations within the competitiveness equation may be ascertained. Until these two steps have been taken, discussions of competitiveness and the environment will continue to remain theoretically based, unfounded in field research. Much will undoubtedly depend on the firm and sector. In the case of the European chemicals industry, the high concentration of German firms will

---

[54] *Competitiveness in Industry: A First Approach* (Brussels: Eurostat, Panorama of EU Industry Supplement, 1995), pp. 77–84.

lead to assessments of competitiveness being focused more closely on domestic competition. In the case of iron and steel, British Steel faces little domestic competition, and therefore looks to European and extra-EU competitors to assess its competitiveness. Once principal competitors are singled out, the details of cost competitiveness, price competitiveness and marketing competitiveness can be targeted.

For discussions of trade and the environment, it is necessary to move to more aggregated analysis using trade data to assess international competition. At the sectoral level the data reveal certain patterns, but these patterns obscure firm-level activities. For this reason, quantitative trade data research needs to be supported by firm-level qualitative interviews. In this way, the degree to which patterns of trade can be attributed to environmental factors may begin to be established. Qualitative analysis may also begin to unravel the high intra-firm component of international trade which complicates foreign trade indicators. With pollution abatement costs running at below 5% of total production costs, the suggestion that environmental regulations are shaping international trade patterns (purely because environmental issues have been pushed on to the business agenda recently) is misleading. Rather than overarching generalizations regarding environmental regulations and production and trade, there is a need for case study analysis to assess the extent to which firms are responding to regulations, the extent to which this affects competitiveness, the extent to which firms are proactive or reactive, and the extent to which they see regulations still as costs rather than benefits within their corporate strategies.

However constructed, firms are most likely to respond to increased competition by lowering costs per unit output or by creating additional value-added per unit of output (through product development or customer service). Until the environmental component of these responses can be extracted, such as the lowering of energy costs (thereby reducing emissions) or the development of 'green' products, the linking of competitiveness and environment will continue to be problematic, and possibly misleading. With several publications now providing information on a broad range of competitiveness indicators, even to the extent of ranking countries according to the figures, environmental indicators will slowly emerge but will need to be treated with caution.

One may conclude that environmental competitiveness is unclear as a concept. However, within the environment industry – incorporating environmental goods and services for industry, including end-of-pipe technologies and cleaner technologies – there has been an explosion of activity in the 1980s and early 1990s. In this industry one can utilize the concept more explicitly.

If the environment is to be considered significant within competitiveness indicators, pollution abatement costs must be higher than at present. Where the environment becomes important is in innovation. If one follows the Porter argument that regulations lead to innovation, one can credit the developments of end-of-pipe technologies, and the more recent transition to process and production methods of contamination reduction, to regulations. In this way, regulations have played an important part not only in controlling emissions and waste, but in promoting the development of efficient industrial technologies.

Investment and environment

While the link between competitiveness and environment has been made only recently and remains unclear, that between investment and environment has been well explored within the academic community. The ecological argument that promoted the research into the phenomenon of investment flows along gradients from sites of strict regulation to sites of low regulation runs as follows. Firms initially sought locations of low regulation in order to reduce pollution abatement costs and to gain competitive advantages from the avoidance of such costs – the so-called 'pollution haven' hypothesis. Higher intensities of pollution from such firms, essentially those located in developing economies, gave rise to the need for increased regulation, much of it triggered by international environmental pressure. This resulted in the flow of regulatory frameworks to these developing economies. Following from these regulatory frameworks was the need for environmental industry goods and services, imported from developed economies – the source of the multinational polluters and regulatory frameworks. This triple process of industrial intervention in the developing world was expressed as the export of pollution from North to South. This argument is supported by many environmentalists.

To prove the first of these steps – the flow of foreign direct investment into developing economies in order to produce 'pollution-intensive' products – numerous studies took place dating back to the late 1970s. The bulk of these took place in the United States where industrial data were sufficiently disaggregated to ascertain the investment decisions of firms and the extent to which there was indeed a flow of investment that could be attributed to stricter environmental regulations. One of the few studies that revealed a movement of investment in order to produce in less regulated locations concerned the US chemicals industry; however, this movement was within the United States, rather than international. Research reveals that environmental regulations do not rank among the important factors in location decisions: traditional factors such as materials, labour and markets remain central. Therefore it may be said that, based on the evidence, environmental regulations have had no systematic effects on the size of the search area for relocation, the number of sites seriously considered, the size of the facility built or the decision to expand an existing plant rather than build a new plant.

The problems in revealing that international investment decisions are made in response to environmental regulations are numerous. Clearly, there are several case studies that reveal that low-regulation environments have been recipients of polluting industries; these we can call the 'Bhopal cases'. Having justifiably received considerable international attention, these cases have been highlighted as the tip of the iceberg of North–South 'pollution-intensive' investments. The research to date provides little evidence that this iceberg is at all large.

There is more evidence to reveal that pollution intensity rests with domestic producers within the South rather than as a consequence of multinational investment. This statement, however, has to be deconstructed. There is evidence at a case study level of considerable outsourcing and contracting out of the 'dirty' elements of the production process by multinational firms. In this way they are able to maintain a cleaner image, distancing themselves from heavily polluting practices. The outcome of such a reorganization of production leads only to the displacement of pollution, on to those domestic firms with fewer resources for which pollution abatement costs might prove impossible to bear. Clearly, these suppositions require more detailed research.

The counter-argument to that of out-sourcing and the buying in of ready-made 'dirty' products is that put forward by many in business: that multinational firms have become highly aware of environmental pressures among international movements and individual consumers, and that they have implemented globalized standards. This suggests that the 'Bhopal cases' have been lessons learned; firms such as Union Carbide would now institute the same equipment and procedures in a plant in India as they would in North Carolina. This argument goes one step further. Because many multinationals have recently expanded production to developing countries, for reasons of domestic markets rather than low regulation, they have invested in state-of-the-art plants and equipment that exceed the standards of those in place in their developed-world locations. This argument has been termed 'leapfrogging'.

Just as the out-sourcing argument requires research above and beyond a limited number of case studies, so does the leapfrogging argument. At present it is unclear to what extent these processes are being carried out and to what extent different processes are taking place in different geographical regions; for instance, it may be the case that India has experienced different multinational strategies from those employed in Mexico. A problem that researchers face in attempting to unravel these arguments is making the separation between managerial rhetoric and company environmental statement (generally, that the firm is 'working harmoniously with the environment') and actual company strategies and practices and the achievement of environmental objectives.

Regulatory push or pull?

To answer the two questions set out in the introduction, it must be systematically proven that environmental regulations lead to a 'race to the bottom' (down the gradient to low-regulation locations) or that they can attract investment and, via trade, affect regulations elsewhere. Current research does not support either of these propositions. There are studies of particular cases where particular patterns may be observed, but there is little or no systematic change in operation. The principal difficulty is that of assessing the impact of environmental regulations within the investment and competitiveness decisions of firms relative to other factors. At present, the environment is not a key factor in these decisions.

From the 1970s and 1980s, there were suppositions that the inter-nationalization of production and multinational activity would inevitably lead to rational economic decisions by management to seek low-cost production sites. By the same argument, it follows that firms will seek low-regulation locations for production. These suppositions remain unproven and must be considered alongside numerous factors in locational decision-making. It is erroneous to assume that all firms act rationally according to economic necessity, since a complex array of associated factors has to be borne in mind, such as the overall structuring of firm operations internationally, the location of markets, and governmental pressures and favours.

The basic problem behind trade and environment research, which incor-porates the debates relating to competitiveness and investment, is the separation of factors of production and the roles of environmental regula-tion, pollution abatement costs, and technological innovation (end-of-pipe and process and production methods), among others, in industrial location decisions and sales and marketing strategies (e.g. ecolabelling). Beyond the United States, where the industrial census has revealed useful data for environmentally based analysis, the lack of good data is a problem. There is need for solid environmental data in industrial records in order to acquire sufficient information regarding sectoral and national impacts of environmental programmes and strategies relative to associated effects.

Without information on the actual responses to regulations in terms of trade and investment, it is difficult to shape future regulatory frameworks and to understand the ways in which existing regulations are achieving their environmental objectives or leading to international pollution displacement. The role of business, alongside regulatory bodies, not only in formulating regulations but also in implementing strategies, and moni-toring and updating regulations is critical. Only with accepted frameworks will regulations be effective in achieving the goals of cleaner industries, cleaner products and cleaner environments. To achieve this, business must concede the goal of environmentalism, of environmental 'benefits', rather than seeing the environment as a 'cost' or a niche market (similar products, different packaging).

Apart from these difficulties, the environment must be put in its place. While sustainable development requires the environment to be top of the business agenda, it still has not arrived. For example, the 1996 UK DTI white paper on competitiveness[55] barely refers to the environment in its analysis. It does not address the environment specifically among the numerous factors affecting outward investment; it also, for that matter, fails to provide a definition of competitiveness. I refer to this report since it is symptomatic of much research that emanates from public- and private-sector business-oriented research. It might be said that the environment is not central to most firms' strategy meetings unless it is slowing down production (such as state interventions as a consequence of regulatory breaches), giving rise to licensing red tape or offering market advantages, e.g. ecolabelling. Only by stressing that the environment is part of a complex web of strategic factors within a firm can a regulatory framework be accepted and implemented and environmental objectives be achieved.

To say that firms are the stewards of the Brundtland process of environmental sustainability would be misleading, since they are generally unwilling or unable to invest in the long term if such an investment threatens their current competitiveness. It is the role of governments and multilateral agencies, via effectively resourced and monitored international environmental agreements, to enable firms to undertake longer-term environmental investments via regulatory mechanisms that do not jeopardize the short-term competitiveness of firms that are in pursuit of longer-term environmental objectives.

---

[55] Department of Trade and Industry, *Competitiveness: Creating the Enterprise Centre of Europe*, Cm. 3300 (London: HMSO, June 1996).

Discussion

Participants in the discussion following this presentation generally supported the Porter hypothesis, that higher environmental standards can lead to new market opportunities. This may be particularly true for developing economies that are able to leapfrog the dirtier stages of development and invest directly in clean technologies.[56] Similarly, transnational corporations (TNCs) may ensure that their investments in developing countries meet high standards, in the expectation that growing prosperity will lead to a steady rise in public demand for higher environmental quality; if TNC plants did not meet these standards, costly retrofits would be required. The impact of this process on smaller, domestically owned industries, however, was less clear.

More pessimistically, there is a problem with perceptions: even though there is little or no evidence of a reduction in competitiveness deriving from high environmental standards, many businesses and politicians believe that there is, or at least behave as though they believe it. The example of the EU's proposed carbon/energy tax, where implementation was conditional on similar actions by other OECD countries, was cited, as was threats of disinvestment from developing countries tightening up regulations in the mining sector. It is likely that the arguments and perceptions differ markedly from sector to sector; as with the previous topic for debate, more research is clearly needed.

---

[56] See David Wallace, *Sustainable Industrialization* (London: Royal Institute of International Affairs/Earthscan, 1996) for a development of this argument.

Chapter 3

Industry Concerns

This session of the conference included an introduction by the chair, six presentations and the normal exchange of questions and views. For ease of reading, these have been grouped together in this report into four sections. The first deals with perspectives from different sectors of industry, drawn primarily from the presentation by **David Wakeford** *(chemicals), with additional contributions from* **John Canning** *(timber),* **William Seddon-Brown** *(waste) and* **David Wallis** *(transport) interspersed at appropriate points. The remaining sections look in more detail at particular aspects of industry concerns from different perspectives: process and production mechanisms (Charles Arden-Clarke), developing country issues (Veena Jha) and trade and climate change policies (Duncan Brack). The final section summarizes the wide-ranging discussion which followed all the presentations.*

3.1 Industry perspectives

David Wakeford began by stressing two main themes. The first is the importance of economic growth to improve the global standard of living and to provide the conditions and finance to enhance environmental protection. Economic growth has been facilitated for almost fifty years by the fivefold growth in freer and fairer international trade underpinned by the GATT rules, and more recently by the WTO (see Figure 3.1).

Second, as living standards have improved and environmental awareness has increased, there has been a significant move towards greater environmental protection – a world-wide trend. This, together with technological development, has stimulated moves towards cleaner processes, more effective management of raw materials, energy and waste, as well as the manufacture of more environmentally friendly products. These changes, sought by society, must be financed in what is an increasingly

Figure 3.1: Trade liberalization and the growth of world trade: world merchandise trade index, 1945–2005

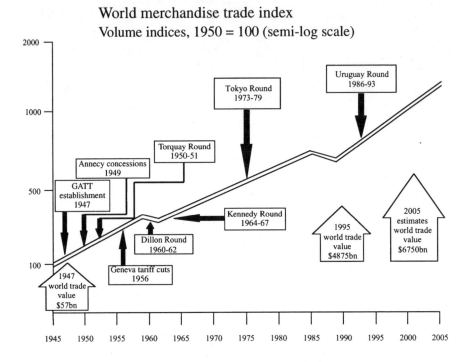

World merchandise trade index
Volume indices, 1950 = 100 (semi-log scale)

competitive market place. Only a profitable and competitive company aware of the contemporary concerns of society can afford to develop and improve its environmental performance towards a more sustainable future.

Economic growth, the opening of national markets and environmental protection are, therefore, largely complementary and compatible objectives – and the relationship between trade and environmental issues is of great importance to industry.

The use of trade measures to achieve environmental improvement

ICI opposes the general use of trade-restrictive measures designed ostensibly to protect the environment. Free trade is an efficient way of utilizing resources and maximizing wealth creation, which are essential factors for sustainable development. Trade restrictions, however, inhibit wealth creation and the efficient use of resources; if they were to become an established way of promoting environmental protection their effectiveness would gradually diminish as international trade itself diminished. If trade were to be linked with environmental issues, why should it not be linked to other areas where it could also be used as an instrument for change? The use of trade measures might easily proliferate not only for environmental improvement, but to create protectionist barriers for commercial reasons. If such a scenario were to develop, international trade and global growth would be severely inhibited, and there would be little or no driving force towards environmental improvement.

Having achieved so much through the GATT, it would be ironic, now that we have the WTO, if environmental measures caused a return to a protectionist and less interdependent world.

International institutions

While in some instances the use of trade measures has successfully achieved environmental objectives, these successes have been achieved primarily because they were focused on actions, as in, for example, the tuna-dolphin dispute. Trade restrictions to achieve environmental objectives are adopted primarily because the present international bodies addressing environmental issues are not able to implement environmental agreements effectively. Environmental issues are addressed by a farrago of international organizations. If there were a more focused and consistent approach, through fewer organizations – or even a single body – with influence, there would be less reason to link trade restrictions to environmental improvement. Such an organization could negotiate more effectively with national governments, as in the case of the WTO, trading a concession in one area with a benefit in another. As environmental issues are so sensitive both politically and emotionally, it would be crucial for such an organization to be equitable in its representation of the interested parties, governments, industry and non-governmental organizations. Its decisions should be based on sound science, and on a pragmatic approach, reconciling economic growth with environmental protection.

Multilateral environmental agreements

There is little doubt that some environmental issues are best addressed through the use of trade measures. ICI supports the use of a limited number of trade measures to address those environmental issues that have a global impact and where multilateral action is essential. The Montreal Protocol (elimination of CFC production), Basel Convention (movement of hazardous waste) and CITES (Convention on International Trade in Endangered Species) are examples of MEAs with trade measures. There are more in the process of formulation (e.g. the UN Framework Convention on Climate Change, or the Prior Informed Consent (PIC) Convention, covering banned and severely restricted goods) and some of those already in place are expanding (e.g. the Basel Convention).

The proliferation of MEAs, however, particularly unfocused treaties, would be unmanageable and, once again, would reduce the effectiveness of trade measures and have an adverse impact on the world economy. There is evidence that some of these measures are already becoming less effective. It is a fact, for example, that a black market in ozone-depleting CFCs has developed which is undermining the Montreal Protocol by delaying the necessary move away from the use of CFCs. Similarly, while the developed world has acted to reduce and eliminate the production of CFCs, developing countries have successfully argued that, as they have not used large quantities of CFCs, they should not be required to comply immediately. This is leading to a rather cynical view in both developed and developing countries about their own obligation to phase out the production of CFCs.

To pick another example, the Basel Convention is now being extended to cover a variety of wastes that were not anticipated. The extension of the Convention to include, for example, metal waste has led to what is seen as unwarranted trade sanctions aimed at developing countries and being imposed by developed countries, limiting valuable recycling opportunities.

At present, each MEA tends to have a different heritage and they do not necessarily conform to GATT rules. They are, therefore, not necessarily consistent in their trade measures. National customs authorities and other government departments have to implement the controls, and business must comply with them. Too many and too complicated agreements will ultimately render MEAs ineffective.

MEAs should be negotiated under UNEP guidance, taking into account WTO views, to achieve a consistent and practical approach. If trade measures are in place, then they have to be understood and effectively enforced. If MEAs were to be implemented in full agreement and cooperation with the WTO, then all the member countries of the WTO would be committed to compliance.

It is important that environmental issues be addressed though fewer international organizations, and that close liaison be maintained between trade specialists and environmental specialists. In the past the disciplines of trade and environment have existed in isolation. This has been the case not only in international organizations, but also with companies. To achieve the correct balance between environmental protection and free trade, environmentalists and trade specialists must address the issues together.

Process and production methods

Dictation of process and production methods (PPMs) by individual governments is not desirable. The banning of selected processes not only would inhibit competition between the processes used for the production of the same product, but could stifle the development of new and sustainable technologies. Provided a process is able to operate within permitted limits covering environmental emissions, then it should be the costs associated with meeting those limits that dictate its long-term viability. The higher the environmental impact, the higher the cost to comply with the environmental protection requirements.

The local imposition of PPM standards on domestic manufacturing industry is obviously a national prerogative, but it should not be used to restrict imported products, whatever the process used for their production. This kind of action would be in conflict with the GATT. If PPMs are included as appropriate measures within an MEA, however, this would be much more acceptable, as their imposition would be multilateral rather than unilateral.

Environmental measures that affect trade

Standards and regulations for environmental protection

Standards and regulations for environmental protection should be based on sound science and a proper understanding of environmental conditions. Some environments are less able to assimilate emissions than others, so global standards are not appropriate. Only where there is a global effect or a cumulative effect are common standards likely to be necessary. Generally agreed guidelines for setting those standards would be useful to harmonize national approaches.

Environmental dumping

Linking trade to the environment can be manna from heaven for those wishing to take a protectionist stance against trade. There is considerable concern that those countries that do not impose environmental standards equivalent to those in the developed countries may have lower relative costs and thereby an unjustified competitive advantage. The answer to this is not to take unilateral action against imports from those countries, but to strive to get them to improve their environmental standards. This can be done by:

- building manufacturing plants in developing countries so that the plants conform with the highest level of environmental performance for similar plants in developed countries;
- enabling standards of living to improve in developing countries, as a result of which the level of environmental protection should also improve;
- assisting in improved environmental management through training and technology transfer;
- adopting purchasing standards that link purchases to progressive improvement in environmental performance or that conform to the ISO 9000 and ISO 14001 series of environmental management standards.

Product controls

Product controls focus on the chemical composition and physical characteristics of products in relation to their intended use where there is a potential impact on health, safety and environment. They also extend to regulations or voluntary agreements covering the registration, labelling, packaging, storage, movement, recycling and recycled contents of products. The GATT allows countries to impose the product controls they deem appropriate to protect human health and/or their environment, provided these are in compliance with the GATT principles of non-discrimination and national treatment. While product controls are frequently used as instruments for environmental protection, they can also be used primarily as protection for domestic industry.

The application of different product registration requirements for different countries creates trade barriers and causes significant extra costs for imports, thereby distorting trade. Harmonization of registration schemes for chemicals – for example of the criteria for hazard classification – would be a benefit to both companies and health, safety and the environment.

Ecolabelling schemes are of particular concern as they can be misleading and confusing. Different national schemes are rarely based on the same criteria and tend to be designed around domestically produced goods. If not based on sound science and full life-cycle assessment, they may also lead to resource misallocation and inappropriate environmental policies. An example is refrigerators containing ICI's ozone-benign refrigerant.[57] These are not eligible for an ecolabel despite the fact that recovery and recycling of the refrigerants would prevent any climate change impact, and also despite their higher energy efficiency, reducing the demand for energy. Refrigerators containing hydrocarbons, in contrast, are allowed an ecolabel even though the refrigerant is both flammable and a regulated volatile organic compound (VOC). This ecolabel, despite being voluntary, is a distinct barrier to trade.

---

[57] Hydrofluorocarbons (HFCs), which are non-ozone-depleting, but are greenhouse gases.

[*William Seddon-Brown* made the additional points that it was important to involve all stakeholders in the process of developing criteria; that a self-declaration scheme should be adopted; and that, if there is to be a harmonized EU ecolabelling scheme, then national schemes should eventually be phased out.]

Mutual recognition agreements covering product requirements do exist; the OECD has had mutual acceptance of data for many years. However, their implementation is variable. Many common standards have been agreed over recent years; it is important that they are extended and applied internationally to reduce costs and bureaucracy. The WTO, the International Standards Organization (ISO) and other international organizations should monitor schemes currently in place and ensure that they are not used for purposes of commercial protectionism.

Environmental management

William Seddon-Brown made the following points on the main principles to be followed in the development of environmental management standards (EMS): the adoption of such standards should use industry experience and 'buy in'; it should remain voluntary; EMS should be compatible with other management systems and consistent with regulatory approaches; they can achieve public credibility by appropriate and flexible methods of verification; they should avoid prescription, but focus on performance; and they must take shareholder expectations into account. He supported the development of a single set of international EMS, preferably based on the ISO 14000 series. It was important to ensure that newly developed standards do not reduce flexibility or create barriers to trade.

Fiscal and economic instruments

Some countries apply taxes on emissions or products with the aim of reflecting the full environmental cost on manufacturing industry. Border rebates are allowed for taxes on products or raw materials but not for taxes on processes, such as emission taxes. Therefore, those taxes, applied nationally and not subject to border tax rebates, cause higher product costs and make domestic industry less competitive in export markets. If these taxes are aimed at environmental problems that are cross-border or global, then to avoid distortion of competition there should be an agreed multilateral approach, rather than unilateral national measures that do little to resolve the overall problem.

The granting either of general subsidies or of subsidies specifically aimed at environmental improvement does not necessarily help in the long term. When given to support exports, subsidies fundamentally distort trade and do not encourage the production of goods in countries able to produce those goods most cost-effectively. Subsidies given for industrial production (not including research), while alleviating short-term financial problems, shelter businesses from commercial reality and enable the continued survival of processes that would not survive in a normal competitive market situation. Subsidies do not assist in establishing a competitive and fully sustainable approach to production and trade.

Developing country concerns

Developing countries have real concerns that trade measures linked to environmental issues will be used as barriers to their trade with developed countries. These concerns should be taken seriously, especially since tariff barriers have now been substantially reduced. Developing countries' economies should be stimulated through international trade; as a result, their environmental standards will also improve. While developing countries are concerned about barriers against their goods, the converse is also true: there is evidence that developing countries themselves are using environmental measures as barriers against imports from the developed world.

Transport industry concerns

David Wallis summarized his concerns over the future development of trade and environment policy as follows.

Although I fundamentally believe that government, industry and consumers must have a shared interest in ensuring that environmental standards are met in the most economic and efficient way, speaking for my own industry, it is difficult to detect the signs of that shared vision in reality. At a global as well as local level, there is still significant fragmentation and inconsistency which unless resolved will cause implementation to falter or even fail. What is needed is a proper framework to establish common principles, approaches, standards and targets, which can be applied globally, not simply industry- or region-wide, to avoid the risk of inhibiting global GDP growth, limiting the aspirations of developing countries and stifling innovation and progress at birth.

Such a framework would contain a number of key principles:

- Global authorities must set policy, objectives and goals.
- Criteria for policy formulation must include cost–benefit analyses, economic, social and environmental factors.
- The choice of solutions and policy instruments must result from a partnership consensus between authority, industry and consumers – the recent European auto-oil programme is a prime example of effective partnership.
- Decisions must be based on sound science and available data.
- Implementation of policy must not harm global competitiveness and should rely on incentives rather than penalties.
- The process must be transparent with open consultation leading to consistent long-term policies with clear defensible objectives.
- Policy must be easy to administer, implement and monitor.

With such a framework in place, the next concern is to choose the most effective mix of the three main policy instrument options to achieve environmental goals:

1. Regulating norms and standards:
   - most widely used to date; effective but costly;
   - focus has been on end-of-pipe emissions;
   - often bureaucratic, requiring considerable enforcement and administration;
   - inflexible, providing little incentive for exceeding standards.

2. Voluntary initiatives:
   - several successful examples;
   - require cooperative dialogue between authorities, communities and local industry;
   - depend on dialogue and transparency as the basis to establish mutual trust.
3. Environmental economic instruments:
   - include demand-side management, tradeable permits, emission charges, taxes;
   - utilize market mechanisms by linking price to environmental aim and impact;
   - require good understanding of the cost of externalities;
   - encourage innovation and technology solutions.

Each situation or industry has different problems and potentially requires different solutions, and the key must be to select the best mix of these instruments to achieve collective environmental goals in the most efficient way.

In my view, industry fully understands and supports the vision of sustainable growth, in which economic and environmental objectives can be reconciled. But we do have very real concerns that governments seem to see the imposition of draconian economic or regulatory instruments as the only way to force industry to develop the technological solutions that are needed to solve the problems. Of course, technology can provide much of the solution, but not all. And even those solutions are much more likely to flow from positive encouragement than from restrictions and penalties. I am convinced that collectively we can find the right solutions, by relying on a prudent mix of environmental policy instruments, tailored to deal with the specific issues and circumstances in a particular area, which support the key principles within the framework I described earlier, and which are founded in a partnership between all the key stakeholders.

I close by encouraging policy-makers to think positively and twice, before they risk killing off the golden goose of industry – which is frankly the only realistic source of the solutions we all seek.

Work of the WTO Committee on Trade and Environment

The speakers accepted that the CTE is undertaking a valuable role in assessing the relationship between trade and environment. *William Seddon-Brown* concluded by suggesting the following framework of principles for the Committee's further work:

- It should be recognized that economic development promotes improved environmental status.
- Trade measures for environmental purposes should be limited.
- Import and export laws should not be used to enforce practices in other countries.
- Agreements should be used to define standards, not restrictions.
- All legislation should be transparent and take into account economic interests.

3.2 Process and production methods
Charles Arden-Clarke[58]

This paper is about process and production methods (PPMs) and their significance for sustainable development, and about the need for the international community to address this issue. In an increasingly global economy, it is likely that a similarly global approach will be needed to address successfully the negative social, ecological and economic effects of many of the PPMs that predominate today – but a global approach that is also sensitive to the range of needs and priorities of different communities. This paper shows why PPMs are central to securing sustainable development, and briefly outlines how NGOs, including the World Wide Fund for Nature (WWF), could and are addressing this issue.

[58] I wish to thank Martin Abraham, Manus van Brakel, Aimée Gonzales, Nadine Keim, Caroline LeQuesne, Cecilia Oh, Gordon Shepherd and Ana Toni for comments on earlier drafts of this paper. This paper is an adaptation of a discussion paper produced prior to the Singapore Ministerial Conference of the WTO. The views expressed are my own.

The problem

The globalization of the world economy was initiated by the creation of the General Agreement on Tariffs and Trade. The GATT was a revolving contractual agreement between governments, erected in honour of economic efficiency and comparative advantage. In 1947 these two beacons offered light to a world recently ravaged by war, stalked by poverty and driven by suspicion between countries. Through free trade, regulated by this agreement between those same countries, it was hoped that once again all the people of the world could find decent livelihoods.

Simple rules were made to guide this trade – rules that, in addition to preventing arbitrary discrimination between identical products from different GATT members, required that there be no trade discrimination between identical products made using different PPMs. But the world's economy, and indeed its ecology and human society, were not that simple in 1947, and certainly are far more complex now. The understanding of this is growing, from grassroots to senior government levels, as is the realization that new economic policies and rules are needed to reflect this complexity, and to direct the world towards sustainable development.

A part of this complexity was reflected in the GATT from the very beginning. Article XX of the founding agreement provides for exceptions even to the golden rules. Exceptions to protect human, animal and plant life and health; to protect human morals, to conserve 'exhaustible' natural resources, and, perhaps most interestingly, to define products produced by prison labour as 'unlike' other, physically identical, products not so made.

That is the point where the importance of how a product is made, of its 'process and production method', was first recognized in the GATT. In this case it was a recognition that an unfair price advantage could be gained on world markets by exploiting captive labour. It was considered that the immorality of the practice, and the temptation to succumb to it because of the substantial reduction in production costs it allowed, constituted an advantage so unfair that it could undermine the whole trading system. Hence the exception to allow differential treatment of goods produced by prison labour.

Since that time the understanding has grown that, with increasing numbers of people on the planet, the question of *how* they make a living has become crucial to their ultimate survival. Unless the economic activities that generate wealth are conducted with careful regard for the environment and natural resources on which we all ultimately depend, the livelihoods generated will undercut life itself. Furthermore, unless the wealth generated is distributed equitably between people and generations, social, economic and environmental justice within and between nations is threatened.

These realities were recognized in the concept of sustainable development, formulated in the report of the World Commission on Environment and Development in 1987 and subsequently elaborated in Agenda 21, signed at the UN Conference on Environment and Development (UNCED), the 'Earth Summit', in 1992. In the negotiating processes that led up to those two meetings, both governments and civil society gradually came to understand the implications of sustainable development – in particular, that one cannot separate human welfare from the welfare of the planet, and that national and international policies must be coordinated and integrated to safeguard both. Securing human development (increasing human welfare) and protecting the environment were seen to be inseparable necessities, not alternatives.

The understanding that was developed during the UNCED process led in many cases to proposals for policy reforms which centred on changing PPMs – on changing how economic enterprises are conducted, so as to make them sustainable in social and environmental terms. Much of that understanding is now enshrined in Agenda 21. For example, Chapter 8 on 'Integrating Environment and Development into Decision-Making' incorporates sections on choosing how one undertakes economic activities, and on ensuring that the social and environmental costs of those activities are fully accounted for, or 'internalized'. Chapter 14 on 'Sustainable Agricultural and Rural Development' sets out policies that support farmers employing those particular methods of agricultural production that husband natural resources and protect the environment while feeding people. In Chapter 30, on 'Strengthening the Role of Business and Industry', actions are set out for the private sector that would lead them to adopt 'cleaner production' methods, and to account fully for the social and environmental costs of their activities.

This has not happened in the context of the GATT, which in 1995 became the World Trade Organization (WTO), where the issue of PPMs has always been very polarized between North and South. In this context, environment and development have become separated, and are even seen as being in conflict. Yet in reality many of the PPMs that are bad for the environment are also bad for development. If the PPM issue is not addressed in the WTO, it will play into the hands of those who currently profit from environmentally damaging and poverty-enhancing PPMs, while undermining those individuals, countries and companies that adopt sustainable PPMs.

Some examples from real life

A forest that is clear-cut instead of selectively felled represents a loss not only of biodiversity, but of livelihoods. Local and indigenous communities are deprived of the timber if the devastated forest fails to regenerate, and also of the non-timber resources such as medicinal plants, fruits and wild animals that are a source of food or income; the farmer downstream from the forest has his crops washed away by ensuing floods; the fish stocks of coastal fishing communities are depleted by sedimentation of inshore waters and reefs. The economic impacts on others and the increase in poverty resulting from clear-felling a forest can be more significant in sustainable development terms than the loss of biodiversity. Yet the enterprise that fells the forest in this way reaps a larger financial profit, and will be more competitive in world markets regulated by WTO rules.

The pollution from a chemical factory not only kills the fish in the river, but also makes the water unfit to drink for the human community that lives downstream from the factory. Like the farmer and fisherman below the forest, members of that community bear the costs of the PPM but almost none of the benefits, unless they work in that factory. Their health suffers and they may even lose livelihoods based on the resources provided by the river. In this way the wrong PPM can widen the inequities in income distribution within and between countries. Yet those who own the factory will reap a larger financial profit, and will be more competitive in international trade shaped by the WTO.

Even labelling schemes, which indicate to consumers that traded goods have been produced in socially acceptable or ecologically friendly ways, may soon fall foul of WTO rules. Some countries are manoeuvring in the WTO's Committee on Trade and Environment to open the way to formal WTO challenges to governmental, or even non-governmental, voluntary labelling schemes based on PPMs. Fair trade labels such as that of Max Havelaar for coffee, others for socially and ecologically friendly bananas, organically grown food and sustainably produced timber are consequently under increasing threat from the WTO.

The only place where the PPM issue appears in the report of the WTO's Committee on Trade and Environment is where it has been raised by governments that are trying to attack PPM-based ecolabelling, including voluntary ecolabels. In the vacuum left by NGOs, governments are doing what they want concerning PPMs – in this case, defending a domestic forestry industry which in many places employs environmentally destructive forestry practices.

One of the main reasons for the absence of agreement is that those from the South fear the prospect of a new kind of protectionism cloaked in environmental or social concern. Imports from developing countries could be discriminated against on the real or imagined basis that the PPMs in that country were more environmentally damaging or socially unjust.

This is a real concern for the South, given the record of Northern countries on using trade restrictions simply to protect domestic industry. However, it should not paralyse international civil society on the issue of PPMs. In an ever more rapidly globalizing economy, with new investment liberalization agreements following hot on the heels of ever more numerous and powerful free trade agreements, it is imperative that those in all countries with the dirtiest and, for them, the cheapest PPMs are not allowed to be the most competitive. Otherwise the globalization process will help drive many of the world's people into poverty, and its environment to destruction.

A way forward

Doing something about PPMs will first require examining how, in specific cases in different countries, the wrong PPMs both undercut development prospects and damage the environment. It will require working at all levels – local, national and international – and in far more forums than just the WTO. Again, budding investment agreements, such as the Multilateral Agreement on Investment being negotiated in the OECD, are a case in point. National governments and industry both have a responsibility to act on PPMs, but one that in many cases they will still have to be held to by public-interest NGOs. NGOs themselves can act on PPMs, as exemplified by some of the social and environmental labelling schemes that have emerged recently.

In this process of examination, NGOs might wish to prioritize discussions about North–South charged PPM issues, such as the WTO dispute on shrimp and turtles (see Section 2.2, Case H). These are the kind of disputes that can wreak most havoc on NGO as well as governmental cooperation; they are often also those that have the most negative impacts on prospects for sustainable development.

Moving beyond the examination stage on PPMs will require not only working on the sustainable alternatives, but also strengthening the safeguards against trade protectionism masked by environmental or social concerns. It will require working on securing the finance and technology for all countries to have the means to address unsustainable PPMs. And it will require that the needs and concerns of the poorer sectors of society are also met by the solutions to PPM problems. In essence, it will be about defining how PPM problems can be solved in the interests of all people. This will require having no preconceptions about the instruments necessary to solve the problem, but rather bearing in mind the ultimate objective of finding the best sustainable development solutions.

WWF will continue to work in a range of international forums, and at national and local levels, to ensure that both legal and economic frameworks encourage rather than discourage the selection of environmentally and socially sustainable PPMs. In the WTO, we will continue to track the deliberations of the Committee on Trade and Environment, and will follow, publicize and input to formal trade disputes on trade and environment (such as the shrimp-turtle dispute) to illustrate the need for reform of WTO rules on PPMs. In the International Standards Organization (ISO), WWF will continue to seek ecolabelling standards whose primary objective is the development and application of ecolabels that yield environmental benefits by harnessing market forces. In global and regional trade agreements such as the WTO, the European Union and the Asia-Pacific Economic Community (APEC), we will work to ensure that environmental policies that specify sustainable PPMs are not undermined by those agreements. And in the Expert Panel on Trade and Sustainable Development, established with funding from eight government donors, the 18 panellists are developing innovative packages of trade-related policies to introduce sustainable PPMs in key traded sectors such as timber, textiles and electricity generation. WWF has also initiated local-level projects on the sustainable production of traded commodities, including cotton and aquacultured shrimps, which are moving into their second phases.

Multiple solutions in many different forums will be required to find and apply sustainable PPMs in an increasingly globalized economy. All participants in the debate are potential partners for WWF as we seek the policy and market tools to secure PPMs and, in turn, our collective future.

3.3 Developing-country perspectives
Veena Jha

Key issues

Regarding the effects of environmentally related technical regulations on market access, the following questions arise:

1. Do developing countries face particular market access problems because of such standards and regulations?
2. Are environmental standards and regulations any different from other standards and regulations, thus requiring special scrutiny?
3. Is it possible to develop some general principles which could be used in the design of environmental regulations in order to safeguard existing market access?
4. What is the mix of national and international policies that may be required for safeguarding market access, particularly for developing countries?
5. Since adhering to harmonized international standards will necessitate the widespread diffusion of environmentally sound technologies (ESTs), what innovative mechanisms can promote such diffusion?

Rationale for examining market access issues

The adverse effects of environmental measures on market access and competitiveness are likely to be differentially felt by developing countries for a number of reasons, such as lack of infrastructural and monitoring facilities, limited technology choices, inadequate access to environment-friendly raw materials, lack of information, the significant number of small-scale exporters and the emergence of environmental standards in sectors of export interest to developing countries. Moreover, trading opportunities generated by environmental measures may be more advantageous for developed rather than developing countries as exploitation of these new market niches requires skill- and technology-intensive products.

Furthermore, packaging, recycling or other environmental requirements may generally result in unequal competitive opportunities for exporting and importing countries. Such requirements may make little sense in the context of the domestic environmental problems and priorities of the exporting country. However, in so far as these regulations relate to consumption externalities, their fulfilment should be regarded as an essential condition for doing business. Specific problems may arise in cases where these requirements, for example packaging regulations, conflict with the maintenance of the quality of the product, or where stipulations of the importing country result in sub-optimal environmental choices in the exporting country.

While to a certain extent the effects of environmental requirements on trade may be similar to, or exacerbate those arising from, constantly changing conditions in the market-place, such as changes in technology, consumer preferences, price and availability of raw materials, it can be argued that in many aspects environmental requirements are different from other factors such as product quality or fashion. For example, environmental requirements, especially those related to PPMs, may be based on specific values, and pressure groups may be especially vocal on issues of environmental protection, even outside their own countries.

Environmental measures also depend to a significant extent on the use of the precautionary principle and on risk assessment techniques which may, according to the OECD, be 'highly specific to the country or countries making the decision'. It is to be noted that the SPS Agreement, for example, which incorporates some elements of these two principles, recommends that national standards be based on 'scientific principles and not maintained without scientific evidence'. The process of risk assessment may be so complicated and expensive that countries may decide to ban the use of a product or substance on the basis of the precautionary principle. This implies that the scope of protectionist abuse in the case of environmental measures may be greater than in other cases. Moreover, it may often be difficult to judge the 'risks that non-fulfilment may create'. These decisions are often political ones, firmly entrenched in the country's priorities, social preferences, level of development and NGO pressures.

The use of PPM-based mechanisms, in particular, needs special safeguards. PPM-based standards can act as non-tariff barriers to trade for many reasons. Their costs of compliance may be high; the technologies and raw materials required may not be available domestically; the standards may be inappropriate in the conditions of the exporting country; and they may result in the extraterritorial application of the environmental policies of the importing country.

Effects of environmental policies on market access

While generalizations on the effects of developed-country environmental policies on the market access of developing countries are difficult, there is evidence showing that such policies do affect market access in specific markets and specific sectors. Examples from Asian countries' experiences can be found below. In fact, no technical regulation or standard covered by the TBT Agreement, whether related to the environment or not, is expected to have generalized effects on market access. They affect only some products from some sectors and affect some countries more than others. Thus, as for other technical regulations and standards, it may be necessary to have some rules or guiding considerations in place that will safeguard existing levels of market access.

Proposed solutions

Principles could be developed for consideration in the design of environmentally related technical regulations. Such principles could include transparency, proportionality (implicit in the notion of least trade restrictiveness), equivalency and mutual recognition. General principles could also be developed that relate to the trade effects of environmental policies, for example concepts such as the risks that non-fulfilment may create, and the concept of equality of competitive opportunities. Special consideration could also be given for products mostly originating from small-scale firms.

Concerning the role of additional market access in generating trade and environment benefits, key questions that arise are:

• In which sectors would additional market access be specially beneficial?
• What mix of national and international policies would be required to create the enabling conditions that could maximize the chances of additional market access being translated to trade and environmental gains?
• What are the coverage and scope for the usage of clauses relating to special and differential treatment to obtain additional market access for developing countries?

Special reference in this regard can be made to tariff escalation. Tariff escalation should be distinguished from high nominal tariffs, as the effective rate of protection can be high even with low nominal tariffs. If the example of textiles and clothing is considered in this context, it appears that the effective rate of protection for this sector is relatively high in most developed countries. While reducing tariff escalation would not result in direct environmental benefits, it would provide developing countries with an opportunity to increase their exports and thus provide them with incomes to invest in environmental improvements. Whether environmental improvements actually accrue is an open question and will depend on the environmental policies in place. However, while the WTO does not have any jurisdiction on the environmental policies of countries, it does have the possibility of providing better market access.

The notion that income effects are of overwhelming importance in the context of developing countries is borne out by empirical evidence.[59] Better access to markets not only generates income, it may also generate the use of better technologies and product development, all of which can be environmentally beneficial. Moreover, higher incomes and greater developmental opportunities generated through trade would result in changes in social preferences in favour of a better environment. This change in social preferences would have a significant effect on environmental protection.

Removing tariff escalation together with non-tariff barriers is also likely to restore production in accordance with comparative advantages. According to the Brundtland Commission report, producing in accordance with comparative advantage is much more likely to be environmentally beneficial than otherwise. Specific market access commitments that can help create opportunities for environmental protection can be examined on a sectoral basis. The Agreement on Textiles and Clothing could provide useful pointers in this direction. For example, certain implementation schedules can be accelerated to provide greater market access and a better opportunity for environmental protection.

Finally, on the issue of how removing trade restrictions and distortions can yield both trade and environment benefits, several points can be addressed, including:

- In the process of moving to environment-friendly trade patterns, are trade distortions a barrier to environmental improvements?
- Is it possible to develop a taxonomy of conditions under which removing such distortions could result in environmental improvements?
- Is there scope for international trade rules in providing the enabling conditions for the removal of such distortions?
- Are the effects likely to be uniform across developing countries and is there scope for removing such distortions under the present coverage of international trade rules?

---

[59] Gene M. Grossman and Alan B. Krueger, 'Environmental Impacts of a North American Free Trade Agreement', in Peter M. Garber (ed.), *The Mexico–US Free Trade Agreement* (Cambridge, Mass.: MIT Press, 1993).

These are key questions, only some of which can be addressed in this paper.

A central note is that, if appropriate environmental policies are in place, then increased trade can help the environment by generating income, and by invoking the use of better technologies as well as product development. Moreover, higher incomes and better developmental opportunities generated through trade are likely to result in changes in social preferences in favour of a cleaner environment. However, if the required environmental policies are not in place, trade can act as a magnifier of environmental problems. Many developing countries in Asia have recognized this challenge, and have been successful in moving towards improved environmental management, in response to both domestic and external environmental requirements.

While the relationship between trade liberalization and environmental protection is an indirect one, there is more evidence to suggest that trade restrictions or distortions may result in environmental damage. It can be noted that, although the WTO does not have any jurisdiction on the environmental policies of its member countries, reducing trade restrictions falls entirely within the competence of the WTO, and, while several exceptions to trade liberalization are considered as necessary for environmental considerations, there is little discussion on the importance of trade liberalization for environmental purposes.

Technology questions

Is the process of international harmonization of environmental standards working efficiently? What barriers and opportunities are created for developing countries by national and international environmental policies? What is the role of technology diffusion in promoting additional market access and moving to higher environmental standards? There are no definite answers to these questions. The responses are likely to vary among countries depending on, *inter alia*, the nature of the environmental standards and policies involved and the level of economic and technological development of the countries considered.

In response to the first question, two key issues should be noted. First, although international harmonization of environmental standards may be justified and easy to implement in some cases, it has become increasingly clear that in many other cases they are neither desirable nor easily attainable. There are problems associated with the forms of standard setting, and the criteria used do not often appropriately reflect the diversity of markets and producers involved.

Second, the effective implementation of internationally agreed standards is to a large extent dependent on access to the relevant technologies and the capacity of countries or firms to acquire and assimilate such technologies. From recent experiences it is evident that only those countries and firms that have a sufficiently strong technological base to manage changes are in a position to meet the requirements of international environmental standards. The technology issue appears to be critical, especially in the implementation of PPM-related standards where the local capacity to identify the relevant production technology and to acquire, diffuse, assimilate, adopt and, if necessary, upgrade such a technology is an essential condition for realizing production-related international standards. Unfortunately, in the debate on the implementation of national and international environmental policies and standards, little attention is paid to the technological dimension, or to the difficulties faced by developing countries, and in particular their small and medium-sized enterprises (SMEs), in accessing ESTs. But understanding the sources of domestic and international constraints on the transfer, acquisition, utilization, absorption and generation of ESTs is clearly a prerequisite to effective environmental policy formulation and implementation in all countries. The rest of this section will address these pertinent issues, focusing on both technology supply- and demand-side problems and the policy measures that need to be set in motion, at national and international levels, to ease the prevailing constraints.

It is widely acknowledged that meeting the environmental challenge, whether in the national or the international sphere, requires technical change and innovation in the field of ESTs. Indeed, it was in recognition of this fact that the development and transfer of ESTs was given greater importance in the strategy set out in Agenda 21. It was stated that: 'access to and transfer of environmentally sound technology are essential requirements for sustainable development'.[60] Similar declarations supporting the transfer of ESTs to developing countries on favourable terms have been issued by other multilateral environmental agreements. However, despite such statements of intent, the transfer and diffusion of ESTs in developing countries have so far been very modest and the barriers to accessing such technologies are likely to remain formidable. In many respects, the barriers to accessing ESTs are not different from those often faced by developing countries in accessing and transferring other types of technology. A clear understanding of these constraints is indispensable when searching for solutions.

A major constraint common to most developing countries is their limited technology supply capability – although in the last two decades there has been rapid technological and economic development in some countries leading to a growing divergence in technological capability. The implication for the process of transfer of ESTs is that it has a differential effect among developing countries. While the relatively more advanced countries are in a stronger position to generate ESTs and to assimilate ESTs acquired through transfer of technology, other developing countries – indeed, the majority – suffer from limited technology supply capacity. In addition to weak inducements for technological change coming from the demand side, a number of factors constrain the domestic supply of technology in the latter group.

First, most of these countries are deficient in skilled personnel, especially at the technical levels. Many of the low-level absorptive skills that are taken for granted in developed countries are lacking. Consequently, even mundane activities such as identifying relevant technologies, plant layout, production control, maintenance and process optimization call for substantial capability building.

Second, the technological infrastructure necessary to support local capability building and the diffusion of new technologies is often lacking. The process of building local technological capability and the capacity to assimilate, imitate and upgrade technology is a complex process. It often

---

[60] 'Agenda 21: Programme of Action for Sustainable Development', in *Earth Summit, Agenda 21: The United Nations Programme of Action from Rio* (E.93.I.II) (New York: UN, 1993), ch. 34, para. 34.7.

involves far more than gaining access to international technology flows, though clearly such access remains vital. The assimilation, adaptation and further development of internationally acquired technologies such as ESTs require the building of new capabilities that do not exist in developing countries. What determines the development of such capabilities? At the national level, capability development is determined by the policy regime on trade and industry, and by investments in skills, information flows, infrastructure and supporting institutions. At the micro level, it is the outcome of enterprise-level efforts to build technical skills, and firms' capacities to acquire and assimilate new technologies, to adjust to changing market demands (domestic or foreign), and to interact with other enterprises, technology suppliers and supporting institutions such as standards laboratories, extension services, research centres and quality control centres.

Third, small and medium-scale activities predominate in the production and trading sectors of most developing countries. Although SMEs in developed countries have played a leading role in technological changes and economic growth, in most developing countries SMEs are characterized by low technological capacity, lack of finance, low-level skills and poor management structure. As a result, they are often ill-equipped to deal with the challenges posed by technological changes and are highly sensitive to changes that require higher-level skills or incur cost increases.

Experience of developing countries with regard to market access and competitiveness

One of the first attempts to analyse trade and environment linkages in developing countries is being undertaken in the context of the UNCTAD/ UNDP and UNCTAD/UNEP country case studies.[61] In the Asian region, the secretariats of both the Association of South-East Asian Nations

---

[61] Country-specific studies, carried out in around 20 developing countries and countries in transition by local research institutes under the joint UNCTAD/UNDP project on 'Reconciliation of Environmental and Trade Policies' and the joint UNCTAD/UNEP project on 'Capacity-building for Trade and Environment', are *inter alia* analysing factors affecting the relationship between domestic and external environmental policies, standards and regulations and competitiveness. In Asia, the following countries are participating: China, India, Indonesia, Malaysia, the Philippines and Thailand.

(ASEAN) and the UN Economic and Social Commission for Asia and the Pacific (ESCAP) are also undertaking country case studies on trade and environment linkages, and preliminary results of these studies are now becoming available.[62]

Also, to help assess the extent to which developing-country exports are subject to environmental requirements in export markets, the UNCTAD secretariat maintains a database on environmental measures in selected OECD countries.[63] A study that matched this information with trade data for Asian countries, including the Republic of Korea, found that (1) environmental measures tend to concentrate on certain product groups, called in the study environmentally sensitive exports; (2) these environmentally sensitive products are often the subject of multiple simultaneous measures, which makes it difficult to analyse the individual impact of certain environmental measures; and (3) the measures used are different in each market, and the exposure to these is different for each exporting country depending on the export composition.[64]

A number of Asian developing countries have experienced specific cases which have received a considerable amount of attention, such as a German ban on leather and leather products containing pentachlorophenol, affecting India in particular; an Austrian ecolabel for tropical timber, affecting Indonesia, Malaysia and other Asian countries; and boycotts directed against tropical timber originating in Malaysia, Thailand and other countries. Very recently, a US import ban on shrimp (pursuant to a domestic regulation requiring an import ban on shrimp imported from countries which allegedly endanger sea turtles in the process) seriously

---

[62] The ASEAN Secretariat has commissioned country studies on trade and environment linkages from leading research institutes in member states of ASEAN (see ASEAN Secretariat, *ASEAN Workshop Report: Trade and the Environment: Issues and Opportunities*. Manila, Bangkok, Kuala Lumpur, Jakarta 11–23 May 1995, October 1995). Similarly, the ESCAP Secretariat is carrying out a synthesis study based on the experiences of several Asian countries.

[63] The *GREENTRADE* database includes information on prohibitions, standards and regulations, recycling and reuse measures, taxes and charges, deposit/refund schemes, ecolabelling, mandatory labelling, voluntary agreements, government procurement, and substances controlled under the Montreal Protocol.

[64] Roland Mollerus and Rafael Sanchez, 'Environmental Product Policies: Impact on Trade of Selected Asian Economies/Areas', report prepared for ESCAP (UNCTAD, June 1996).

affects Thailand and other countries in the region (see Section 2.2, Case H).

Export-oriented firms in developing countries may need to adjust to environmental requirements emanating from external markets in order to sell in these markets. One concern of many developing countries is that gains arising from recent trade liberalization in certain sectors could be eroded if compliance with environmental requirements were to lead to cost increases or discrimination against their exports. It is also feared that environmental measures may be adopted for protectionist reasons. It should be noted, however, that both the effects of and the responses to emerging environmental requirements differ widely across countries.

An analysis of trade flows shows that there is some ground for such concern in the case of many Asian developing countries (see Box 3.1). Environmental policies and consumer concerns in the developed countries are to a large extent sector-specific, affecting such sectors as fishery and forestry products, leather and footwear, textiles and clothing, and certain consumer products. A number of product requirements, such as bans on the use of specific chemicals and ecolabelling, apply to these sectors. A preliminary analysis indicates that, on average, about one-third of the value of total exports and about half of the value of manufactured exports of developing countries originate in sectors where environmental requirements would be emerging. This may be particularly relevant for Asian developing countries, since over 60% of their manufacturing exports, in value terms, originate in such sectors.

Furthermore, a recurrent theme in studies on the relationship between environmental policies and international competitiveness in the case of developing countries is that adapting to environmental standards may be especially difficult for SMEs. It is to be noted that in many Asian developing countries SMEs account for a very large proportion of total exports. In India, for example, SMEs accounted for 32% of the value of total exports in 1994–5, and this figure was as high as 90% in sectors such as textiles and leather and leather products (sectors where environmental requirements are now emerging).[65] In the Republic of Korea, SMEs also

---

[65] Over 80% of light industrial product exports, such as leather products, garments, plastic products, sports products, crafts and furniture, are produced by small enterprises.

Box 3.1: Environmental policies and market access: sector and scale effects

Environmental policies, standards and regulations may have more significant effects on small firms and in some sectors. In respect of both sector and scale of business, developing countries may be more vulnerable to the adverse competitiveness effects of environmental policies.

Composition of exports

The export drive of many Asian developing countries is based on a relatively small number of sectors and products, indicating early stages of industrialization. Improved market access in these sectors has been negotiated in the Uruguay Round. For example, tariffs in sectors such as pharmaceutical products, steel, farm equipment, furniture, footwear and toys are being reduced. In textiles and clothing, import competition in the developed countries will build up over the ten-year transition period, at the end of which the Multi-Fibre Arrangement will be terminated and the sectors will be reintegrated into the multilateral trading system. Many of the new environmental requirements emerging from the developed countries, however, affect these very sectors.

Scale effects

A large share of the economic activity in Asian developing countries, including in the export sector, originates from the small-scale sector which is relatively more vulnerable to both domestic and international environmental policies for a number of reasons. Some of these reasons have to do with the character of small-scale enterprises themselves, producing low value added products, and facing shortages of skills, technology and finance. In addition, the environmental improvements required to export to developed-country markets may be more onerous for small-scale enterprises because of their greater difficulties in obtaining information, sourcing environmentally friendly raw materials or installing environmentally sound technologies (which may be developed by large-scale firms and can be less easily adapted to small-scale firms); also, the costs of certification and testing of products, etc., would be proportionately higher for small-scale firms.

play an important role (for example, approximately 60% of the electronics exporting units are small-scale). Export strategies are often based on SMEs' large potential for export expansion. In India, for example, this potential can be illustrated by the fact that, while SMEs account for 90% of the exports of textiles, these exports still represent only a small part of total sales. Indeed, much of the recent export growth has come from SMEs, and the same is true for leather products.

Let me highlight some of the difficulties SMEs may encounter when attempting to respond to either domestic or external environmental requirements:

- *High fixed costs.* Fixed costs of installing ESTs may be high for small firms, simply because ESTs may require certain economies of scale.

Even when SMEs install ESTs, it may be difficult to sustain the period of adaptation. There may be a long period between installation and the time when such investments are recovered.

- *High variable costs.* Experience shows that operating costs (even for common effluent treatment plants) may be relatively high for SMEs. In addition, environment-friendly input materials, which may represent a considerable portion of total variable costs, may be expensive. For example, in the leather tanning sector in India, the costs of chemicals required to meet international standards were approximately three times higher than the costs of conventional chemicals. While large firms may use their bargaining power to obtain inputs at competitive prices, this may not be possible for SMEs.
- *Difficulties in passing on costs.* SMEs may find it especially difficult to pass increased costs on to the consumer, because of the highly competitive nature of the markets in which they operate. Large firms may be in a better position to pass on at least a part of the increased costs to the consumer, e.g. because their brand names are well established. Consequently, SMEs tend to be reluctant to take on any cost increases.
- *Lack of finance.* SMEs often cannot themselves finance investment, and credit may not be available for environmental investments. Banks often prefer to lend to larger firms, because of the risk factors.
- *Difficult access to information.* While large firms obtain timely and accurate information directly from importers in developed-country markets and various other sources, SMEs depend on secondary sources, basically government sources, normally entailing considerable time delays.
- *Difficult access to technology.* SMEs may find it difficult to identify ESTs and to incur the costs of acquiring them.
- *Difficulties in obtaining environment-friendly input materials.* SMEs may find it difficult to obtain required input materials (e.g. dyes or chemicals) or to verify their suppliers. Once a new requirement emerges from an external market, a long time often passes before substitutes become available on the domestic market. While large firms may themselves engage in import activities or succeed in persuading their domestic suppliers to switch to environment-friendly materials, such opportunities may not be readily available for SMEs.

Given the above, it is not surprising that many SMEs are often reluctant to incur cost increases in response to environmental requirements, but rather prefer to divert sales to the domestic market or external markets where environmental requirements are less stringent. If this were to happen on a relatively large scale, environmental requirements would have an important bearing on export strategies. Let us take the case of azo dyes, which recently were prohibited in Germany, an important market for small-scale textiles exporters from India. Around 70% of dyes used in India are azo dyes and 25% of these are now banned in Germany; SMEs in India may therefore divert exports from Germany (a 'premium' market) to markets in the Middle East.

While large firms are generally in a better position to respond to domestic and external environmental requirements, they too may encounter certain difficulties on account of a series of factors. For example, the competitive advantage of many developing countries has largely been based on their ability to sell standardized mass-produced products at low prices. Product differentiation is more difficult in the case of homogeneous products, and producers generally find it difficult to recover through price premiums increased costs arising from environmental improvements. In addition, since the home demand for 'environment-friendly' products may be insignificant, the domestic market generally does not allow firms to recover incremental costs. There are other factors that may adversely affect competitiveness, such as lack of environmental infrastructure. Acquiring ESTs may also be relatively expensive for developing-country firms, particularly when intellectual property rights (IPRs) are involved.

With regard to the relationship between external environmental requirements, market access and export competitiveness, I would like to make some additional comments. If exports are significant, governments may introduce domestic regulations which are similar to external regulations, in particular where domestic environmental problems and priorities coincide with those in major export markets. The Indian government has already taken action in the case of benzidine content in dyes, pesticide usage in tea and other agricultural products.[66] It should be noted, however,

---

[66] V. Bharucha, 'Impact of Environmental Standards and Regulations on India's Exports', study prepared for UNCTAD (1994).

that the implementation and enforcement of such regulations may be difficult, in particular with regard to SMEs.

A different situation arises if compliance with external environmental requirements, while entailing significant costs, is of limited environmental benefit to the country of production. Here, incurring such a cost may be a good investment from a commercial point of view – i.e. to maintain export markets – but may yield inferior results from an environmental point of view compared with other investments. For example, a study in the Philippines suggests that a dollar invested in industrial pollution abatement is expected to contribute less to environmental improvement than a dollar invested in basic infrastructure, such as sewage and drainage systems. A study in India also points out that at times there may be trade-offs between addressing domestic environmental concerns and investments in specific environmental improvements in response to requirements emerging from external markets.

Addressing market access and competitiveness effects

The above sections have indicated that environmental policies may have differential effects on developed and developing countries. The relationship between environmental policy, market access and international competitiveness is indeed an important issue for developing countries. Studies carried out in the region show, however, that effects of environmental policies can be addressed by appropriate policies at the national, regional and international levels.

National policies

Country case studies provide examples of government policies to support private-sector-led growth, for example through support for research and development, facilitating the ability of firms to respond to environmental challenges. These policies and measures can, for analytical purposes, be grouped into industrial development policies and macroeconomic policies.

Industrial development policies Case studies have listed a number of examples of policies and measures in this area.

1. *Infrastructural development.* Improvement in environmental infrastructure plays an important role in reducing the costs of compliance, particularly for small firms. For example, improved infrastructure can reduce the cost of compliance with effluent standards. Examples are investments in facilities for common effluent treatment and treatment of hazardous waste.
2. *Testing and certification.* Certification of environment-friendly products may be costly, particularly when producers in developing countries depend on testing and certification bodies in the developed countries. The creation of standardization bodies – or the expansion of existing bodies – in Asian developing countries and steps contributing to their international recognition are of key importance.
3. *Capacity for innovation.* Innovative and cost-saving responses to environmental requirements determine whether compliance costs can be offset or even whether competitiveness improvements can be made. To promote innovation, governments can either provide broad enabling conditions for innovation, or take a more active part in fostering innovation. A study on Malaysia stresses that the central role of technology within Malaysia's development strategy is vital for environmentally sustainable economic growth.[67]
4. *Cooperation between government and industry.* Cooperation of industry with the authorities in the standard-setting process can ensure the design of feasible standards and can facilitate their implementation. Cooperation between government and the private sector has been mentioned as one of the factors explaining Malaysia's success in finding cost-effective solutions for environmental problems. For example, strong cooperation between the government and industry has helped to identify cost-effective approaches for the phase-out of ozone-depleting substances, based on the incorporation of sector-specific elements into a national strategy.[68]
5. *Special measures for SMEs.* Special measures may be needed for some sectors and for SMEs. These could be divided into three categories:

---

[67] Institute of Strategic and International Studies, *Trade and Environment Linkages: A Malaysian Case Study* (Kuala Lumpur: Isis, 1995).
[68] Ibid.

short, medium and long term. In the short run there may be a need to grant more leeway to SMEs in the course of imposing more stringent standards on the sector as a whole. In the medium term, capacity-building, technical assistance and special financing programmes could focus on SMEs.[69] Interim requirements may also permit more leeway for small firms and establishments or for specific sectors such as textiles. Moreover, targeting or prioritization should likewise consider locational factors. In the long run, SMEs in developing countries need to address issues such as lack of financial assistance, lack of technology and the low quality of their products.

One alternative being explored in order to facilitate the adaptation to environmental standards is to encourage the transfer of foreign direct investment to SMEs in developing countries. Finding cost-effective chemicals (e.g. natural chemicals) and reducing the effluent at source in the small-scale enterprises in the textiles and leather sectors could also be undertaken in the long run. Moreover, tax and fiscal incentives could be given to encourage domestic SMEs to invest in environmental improvements. Technological assistance from small-scale units in developed countries to those in developing countries could also be of benefit. In addition, a study on India proposes the following steps for improving the channelling of information and the availability of environment-friendly input materials to SMEs:[70]

- Improve the registration of SMEs so that the government and other agents know where to direct information on environmental requirements.
- Improve the provision of timely and accurate information to SMEs.
- Provide relevant information to suppliers of input materials, such as dyes and chemicals.

---

[69] Experience indicates that larger firms tend to cooperate with one another, e.g. in the exchange of information on existing and emerging environmental requirements in external markets. Capacity-building efforts may help promote a process whereby the know-how and experience acquired by larger firms is transmitted to smaller firms.

[70] S. Das, *The Differential Impacts of Environmental Policies on Small and Large Enterprises in India with Special Reference to the Textile and Clothing and Leather and Footwear Sectors,* study prepared for UNCTAD (May 1996).

- Improve the availability of environment-friendly input materials for SMEs, by providing information, facilitating access to substitutes where they are not supplied locally, supporting research and development or the acquisition of appropriate technology for the domestic production of substitutes.
- Develop domestic regulatory measures or other policy instruments to support the development of environment-friendly substitutes.
- Support the establishment of adequate testing and certification facilities.

Macroeconomic policies To a large extent, integrating trade and environment policies while maintaining international competitiveness requires sustained economic growth and sound macroeconomic and environmental policies. The strong commitment of Asian developing countries to sustained economic growth and openness through the promotion of trade and investment, together with improved environmental management, are key elements of their sustainable development strategies. An important challenge for Asian developing countries is to built further on the synergies between broad economic reform and improved environmental management.

Policies and measures at the regional level

Certain policies and measures could also be developed at the regional level, for example in the areas of technological development; the establishment or further development of testing and certification bodies; the promotion of environment-friendly raw materials, such as environment-friendly dyes; and coordination of approaches to foreign direct investment, *inter alia* with a view to ensuring access to and transfer of environmentally sound technologies.

Policies and measures at the international level

The need to comply with environmental requirements emerging from developed-country markets may increase concerns regarding market access and competitiveness in developing countries. There is a need to take account of certain principles in the design and implementation of environmental policies with significant trade effects. Such principles should *inter alia* include the need to take cognizance of the special conditions and development needs of developing countries, particularly as regards SMEs as well as particular sectors.

In the context of the WTO, the access of developing-country products to the markets of developed countries should be improved. This could include examining how developing countries could benefit from provisions concerning differential schedules for compliance with trade-related environmental measures, such as time-limited exceptions, or the use of a *de minimis* clause.

Diffusion of technologies

In the absence of adequate local supply capability, developing countries will have to rely on the transfer of ESTs from developed countries. However, for many developing countries access to ESTs through international diffusion is neither automatic nor easy. Traditionally, the channels of transfer of technology to developing countries are foreign investment (direct investment as well as other forms such as licensing and management contracts), purchasing technology from foreign suppliers, and overseas development assistance. However, since the mid-1980s, all three of these channels of technology transfer have diminished in importance for most developing countries.

Despite extensive liberalization of investment policies, the actual recorded flow of foreign direct investment to the majority of developing countries in the last decade and half has been small, diminishing both absolutely and relative to foreign investment flows to developed countries. During the same period, many of the developing countries also experienced a fall in their export earnings owing to deteriorating terms of trade and a decline or reversal of capital inflows. As a consequence, developing countries have not been able to sustain the rate of growth of technology imports. Overseas development assistance has also diminished in real terms. All this has intensified the resource gap problem in developing countries. From the above, it is clear that the diffusion of ESTs in developing countries will not be achieved through the traditional channels of technology transfer. There is a need, therefore, to examine the effectiveness of existing multilateral or regional initiatives and mechanisms for transferring ESTs. If existing mechanisms are not viable, new and innovative ways must be found.

If North–South EST flows have not met the needs of developing countries for EST supply, as implied above, then there may be a case for strengthening South–South technology transfer. What are the prospects for South–South trade flows in ESTs?

On the supply side, another barrier to the transfer and diffusion of ESTs in developing countries is the TRIPS Agreement (signed in 1995), which sets out, for the first time, minimum international standards for the protection of the main areas of intellectual property, including patents, copyright, trade marks, industrial designs, geographical indications and layout designs of integrated circuits and trade secrets. Many developing countries are concerned that the full implementation of this Agreement will limit severely the range and volume of technology that they can acquire.

A number of key issues in the area of IPRs/TRIPS and the diffusion of ESTs require further discussion.

- While the TRIPS Agreement was introduced in the context of a multilateral trade discussion that aimed to promote free trade, it is not clear that the standardization of IPRs across national borders has effects that parallel those of free trade. The point is that, while free trade aspires to increase the degree of competition in the international market, the implementation of the TRIPS Agreement in effect implies that firms possessing domestic monopoly power in the use of a particular idea can more easily extend that monopoly power overseas.
- Following the same logic as above, the potential conflict of objectives in the commitments made by governments in the TRIPS Agreement and in the MEAs which encourage the transfer of ESTs to achieve sustainable development need to be explored further.
- While restrictive in many respects, the TRIPS Agreement may benefit inventors in some developing countries. The question is: how can developing countries minimize the restrictive effects of TRIPS while

retaining its positive aspects? One way is by insisting that in future IPRs and the question of dissemination of technical knowledge should be placed within the framework of a pro-competitive strategy. Such a strategy will be compatible with the prevailing free trade orientation and will address the concerns and preoccupations of SMEs.

Conclusions

The debate on environmental policies and competitiveness seems inconclusive at the present time. The dominant view in the developed countries appears to be that at their existing levels environmental policies are unlikely to have significant adverse effects on trade and competitiveness, and that their effects can even be positive. Currently, the competitiveness effects of environmental policies are not an issue of great policy concern. The future impacts, however, may be different if the level of environmental protection is significantly raised.

The developing countries, for their part, are concerned about the implications for international competitiveness and the development of environmental policies. They continue to be particularly concerned that environmental policies, especially when they are based on requirements related to PPMs, may affect market access or be used for protectionist purposes. To an extent, such concern is fuelled by the fact that environmental requirements are emerging in sectors of export interest to developing countries, such as textiles and leather products.

With regard to market access questions, multilateral deliberations and negotiations, particularly in the WTO Committee on Trade and Environment, have important impacts on the international economic and legal context in which developing countries and countries with economies in transition can frame their domestic policies for sustainable development. In a recent non-paper for the Committee by India, the following areas were mentioned as particularly important in the context of environmental policies and market access:

1. safeguarding existing market access conditions against the unwarranted trade effects of environmental policies, for example by taking

account of certain principles in the design and implementation of environmental policies;

2. improving market access conditions, including those for environment-friendly products;
3. removing trade restrictions and distortions, which may result in environmental benefits and contribute to sustainable development.

We have seen that there are many factors determining the market access and competitiveness effects of domestic and external environmental policies, standards and regulations. Among the many firm- or sector-specific factors influencing these are: destination of exports; cost structures; basis for export competitiveness; firm size; relationship with foreign firms; and the availability of raw materials, specialized inputs, technology and information. An examination of these factors indicates that many Asian developing countries may, *a priori*, be relatively more vulnerable to external environmental requirements than other developing regions on account of two factors: the product composition of Asian exports to the developed countries, and the important role of SMEs in existing exports as well as in export promotion policies of many Asian countries.

Having said this, studies also show that competitiveness effects of environmental policies can be addressed – and are being addressed – by appropriate policies and measures at the national and international levels. Many developing countries in Asia have been successful in achieving high export growth rates while moving towards improved environmental management, in response to both domestic and external environmental requirements. This can be attributed to several factors. With regard to policies and measures at the national level, the following can be mentioned:

1. Asia's sustained economic growth and openness to trade and investment;
2. government policies aimed at promoting the development of infrastructure and technology, enterprise development and competitiveness, as well as cooperation with the private sector in finding cost-effective solutions for environmental problems;
3. certain private-sector initiatives.

An important conclusion of empirical work is that SMEs have special difficulties in responding to environmental requirements. At the same time, a study by the Thai Institute for the Environment indicates that there is great potential for improving environmental management in SMEs provided that proper supporting infrastructure is set up. Many practices that are cleaner than present methods of production are feasible for SMEs, but one important obstacle is a lack of knowledge of available options. In this paper I have proposed several measures aimed at improving the access of SMEs to information, ESTs and required input materials such as dyes and chemicals. This is certainly an area where win–win situations can be created through appropriate measures at the national and international level.

To meet environmental challenges without sacrificing the objectives of expanding trade and growth in developing countries, the capacity to adapt, assimilate and develop ESTs is vital to these countries. In the absence of an adequate supply of technologies that may be more appropriate to developing countries, adaptation and access to ESTs assume greater significance. In addition, given the failure of existing mechanisms to facilitate the effective transfer and diffusion of ESTs in such countries, new and innovative mechanisms need to be developed. Some of these have been outlined above.

3.4 Trade and climate change policies
Duncan Brack

This paper aims to outline the implications for international trade of various policy measures that may be taken pursuant to the UN Framework Convention on Climate Change, specifically:

1. the potential use of trade measures within the control protocol to the Convention currently under negotiation;
2. the implications for trade of domestic measures to raise energy efficiency standards for traded goods;
3. the implications for trade of carbon or energy taxes.

Trade measures and the control protocol

A number of multilateral environmental agreements (MEAs) contain trade provisions, i.e. restrictions on trade mandated by or pursuant to the treaty. These have been designed to realize four major objectives:

1. to restrict markets for environmentally hazardous products or goods produced unsustainably;
2. to increase the coverage of the agreement's provisions by encouraging governments to join and/or comply with the MEA;
3. to prevent free-riding (where non-participants enjoy the advantages of the MEA without incurring its costs) by encouraging governments to join and/or comply with the MEA;
4. to ensure the MEA's effectiveness by preventing leakage – the situation where non-participants increase their emissions, or other unsustainable behaviour, as a result of the control measures taken by signatories.

It is conceivable that the negotiators of the climate change protocol may eventually wish to include such measures. A potential model is provided by the 1987 Montreal Protocol on Substances that Deplete the Ozone Layer,[71] which imposes bans on trade between parties and non-parties to the treaty. These trade provisions cover restrictions on both imports from and exports to non-parties of ozone-depleting substances such as chlorofluorocarbons (CFCs), products containing ozone-depleting substances (e.g. refrigerators) and products made with but not containing ozone-depleting substances (e.g. electronic components) – although to date the parties have decided that the introduction of the last category of trade bans is impracticable owing to difficulties in detection. Non-parties that are nevertheless in compliance with the control measures specified in the Protocol are treated as if they were parties.

The negotiators of the Montreal Protocol had two aims in drawing up these trade provisions. One aim was to maximize participation, by shutting off non-signatories from supplies of CFCs and providing a significant

---

[71] For full descriptions of the evolution and operation of the trade provisions, see Duncan Brack, *International Trade and the Montreal Protocol* (London: Royal Institute of International Affairs, 1996).

incentive to join. If completely effective this would in practice render the trade provisions redundant, as there would be no non-parties against which to apply them. The other goal, should participation not prove total, was to prevent industries from migrating to non-signatory countries to escape the phase-out schedules.

All the evidence suggests that the trade provisions achieved their objectives. All CFC-producing countries, and all but a handful of consuming nations, have adhered to the treaty. Although it is difficult to determine states' precise motivations for joining, the trade restrictions do appear to have provided a powerful incentive, and at least some countries have cited them as the major justification. The major CFC producers, mostly located in the United States and western Europe, and therefore subject to the controls from the start, were supporters of the trade restrictions, viewing them as a method of ensuring that the CFC alternatives they produced were not undercut by cheaper competition from non-parties.

Greenhouse gases, of course, are not precisely analogous to CFCs, since most of them – carbon dioxide, some sources of methane, nitrous oxide – are essentially byproducts, whereas others – HFCs, some PFCs – are themselves products that are traded. For this latter group, Montreal Protocol-type trade restrictions could be applied. For the former, and much more important, category, trade restrictions would have to be applied either to the commodities that release greenhouse gases when used – i.e. fossil fuels – and/or to goods made with processes that release greenhouse gases, which in practice means the vast majority of manufactured goods, though there would be obvious detection problems, as with any trade restriction based on a process rather than a product characteristic. Were such trade measures agreed and employed, they would represent a very severe restriction on trade, and an accompanying high welfare loss. By the same token, however, they would create a massive incentive to join and adhere to the agreement; remember, after all, that the Montreal Protocol trade measures have hardly ever been used, since almost every country is now a party to the treaty.

Furthermore, it is possible to conceive of less drastic measures, such as duties or taxes, rather than total bans, applied against various categories of imports from non-parties. Trade measures could be introduced a certain number of years after the protocol comes into force (as in the Montreal Protocol), and/or only after a certain number of parties ratified it, ensuring wide international consensus. Implementation could be tied to reciprocal obligations on the part of the parties – such as the achievement of particular greenhouse gas reduction targets, and/or the removal of trade-distorting and climate-change-accelerating domestic policies, such as agricultural protection or subsidies for energy industries.

It is obvious that such a topic is fraught with difficulty and complexity. It is therefore hardly surprising that very little discussion has so far taken place within the negotiations on measures such as these – though the possibility of trade sanctions was mentioned at the second Conference of the Parties in 1996. It seems unlikely, however, that the agreement can function in the long term without an effective compliance mechanism. There are a limited number of routes by which countries can affect the actions of other countries: military pressure, diplomatic pressure, provision of financial and technological assistance and trade sanctions. It is at least conceivable that, as in the Montreal Protocol, which is an example of a reasonably effective MEA, trade measures may have a role to play as one component of a climate change protocol.

Measures such as these, however, if applied against WTO members, could well be found to be inconsistent with the GATT, following the reasoning of various dispute panel rulings in trade–environment cases over the last five years (although none of these has involved an MEA). The problem is, of course, that trade measures are designed specifically to discriminate between countries based on their membership of the agreement or environmental performance, whereas the essential basis of the GATT is to prevent discrimination in trade. This is not a problem that is unique to the potential climate change protocol; it also applies to other MEAs such as the Montreal Protocol, CITES or the Basel Convention,[72]

---

[72] See, e.g., T. M. C. Asser Instituut, *The Relationship between the Multilateral Trading System and the Use of Trade Measures in Multilateral Environmental Agreements: Synergy or Friction?* (The Hague: T. M. C. Asser Instituut/Ministry of Housing, Spatial Planning and the Environment, 1996); Robert Housman, Donald Goldberg, Brennan van Dyke and Durwood Zaelke (eds), *The Use of Trade Measures in Select Multilateral Environmental Agreements* (Geneva: UN Environment Programme, 1995); and Duncan Brack,

and therefore raises wider questions about the interrelationship between the GATT and MEAs. But once again, if the trade measures were to be successful in their aim of persuading countries to join, they would not be used, and the problem therefore disappears.

Domestic policy measures

Energy efficiency standards

The application of higher minimum standards of energy efficiency to buildings, machinery and products is frequently advocated as a means of mitigating climate change; in the UK, for instance, reductions in energy use of up to 50% are currently technically possible, and reductions of about 20% would be economically justified at current prices. Standards may be decided nationally and/or agreed at an international level. Where they are mandatory, they may be applied both to domestically produced goods and to imports. In the latter case, however, and where they are based on national laws, they possess a potential for creating barriers to trade.

In this case, there are unlikely to be problems with the GATT. In 1994, the US corporate average fuel economy (CAFE) standards for cars were the subject of a GATT disputes panel ruling in a case brought by the European Union after taxes were applied to EU cars imported into the United States which did not meet the standards. The panel ruled that one of the taxes in question – the gas guzzler tax, aimed at all cars with a fuel consumption of less than 22.5 miles per gallon – was GATT-consistent, since it was not applied in a discriminatory way. The CAFE regulations aimed to ensure an average fuel efficiency of 27.5 miles per gallon across the whole of the car manufacturer's fleet. The panel ruled that the application of the regulations only to that portion of the European manufacturers' fleets that was imported into the United States (which tended to be high-value, low-efficiency products) was GATT-inconsistent, since it treated European manufacturers less favourably than US ones. This is a

---

'Reconciling the GATT and Multilateral Environmental Agreements with Trade Provisions: the Latest Debate', *Review of EC and International Environmental Law*, 6:2 (July 1997).

very specific application of efficiency standards, however, and unlikely to be of wide application.

A number of countries maintain differential tariff levels based on efficiency standards, but as long as these apply equally to domestic and foreign producers, there should be no problem with the GATT, under the Agreement on Technical Barriers to Trade. It is conceivable, however, that the progressive raising of efficiency standards may create market access problems, particularly for developing countries. It is also possible that standards, and labelling requirements, may create barriers to trade if it is difficult for exporters to have full access to testing and certification systems to fulfil the conditions required by the importing country.

The research project currently under way at the Royal Institute of International Affairs is designed to look at the experience of these issues in four categories of traded products: cars, personal computers, refrigerators and lighting equipment. My preliminary conclusions are that so far the application of energy efficiency standards has created no real trade or market access problems other than through the administrative barriers associated with testing and certification procedures – where there may therefore be a case for greater international harmonization. The standards themselves are so far either lacking or too low to create any problems.

Energy taxation

An important part of the debate over measures to limit pollution from fossil fuel energy sources relates to the price of energy to its consumers, and whether this reflects the environmental costs caused by its use. The taxation of energy is often promoted as a method of internalizing environmental externalities. There are, however, substantial political difficulties in the implementation of energy taxation, as various political entities – notably the United States and the European Union – have discovered. Relatively few countries have so far employed it, though within the EU Finland, Sweden, Denmark and the Netherlands have all introduced carbon taxes.

One of the major arguments deployed against energy taxation is the impact on international competitiveness of raising domestic industrial

prices. Solutions that have been suggested include adjusting tax levels at
the border, so that exports enjoy rebates equivalent to the level of taxation
imposed, and duties are imposed on imports at levels equivalent to the
taxation they would have been subject to had they been produced
domestically. Under the terms of the GATT, WTO members are permitted
to adjust tax rates at the border inasmuch as these are applied to traded
products. Following various GATT dispute panel rulings, it would appear
that taxes and charges related to processes and production methods cannot
be so adjusted, though the GATT is not completely clear on this and a
Working Party on Border Tax Adjustments in 1970 failed to draw any
conclusion on so-called *taxes occultes* (consumption taxes on materials
and services used in the production and transport of other goods).[73] The
1987 GATT dispute panel on the US Superfund regulations ruled that import
taxes applied to certain chemicals *and to derivatives of them* were permissible, since US chemicals and derivatives were subject to similar taxes. It
has been argued that the same case can be made for energy consumed in
the production process, and that border tax adjustments for carbon or
energy taxes should therefore be permissible. In fact, the Subsidies
Agreement explicitly provides for special treatment for rebating indirect
taxes on energy, fuels and oils used in the production process for *exports*.

There are, however, very severe problems involved with the practicalities of border tax adjustments, including the valuation of the
appropriate level of tax, the likely wide diversity in national tax rates and
the usual detection problems. Again, I am afraid I have no conclusions to
offer at this stage. My own research project is designed to look at the
experience of countries that have introduced carbon taxes, most of which
have exempted industries from their application, and to explore the
arguments around border tax adjustments.

Conclusion

It is difficult to underestimate the importance of the current negotiations
over the control of climate change. The likely failure of most developed
countries to meet even the mild interim target of stabilizing greenhouse
gas emissions at 1990 levels by 2000 means that more drastic action will

be required if climate change is to be tackled effectively. The purpose of the work under way here at Chatham House is to explore the inter-relationship of these policy measures with the multilateral trading system.

3.5 Discussion

A wide-ranging discussion followed these presentations. One general theme was the desirability of a more systematic approach to, and greater predictability in, the setting of environmental regulations; a number of speakers mentioned the need for a single effective 'Global Environmental Organization'. Otherwise, it was feared, environmental law would become a battleground for competing national interests. Another general theme was the need for partnership in resolving trade and environment disputes. Following several years in which different groups had generally failed to understand one another's perspectives, it was felt that the time was now ripe for greater cooperation.

A number of points were made of relevance to developing countries. The automatic link between growing prosperity and improving environmental standards (see Section 3.1) was questioned; it was pointed out that, while this may be true with regard to pollution abatement, it did not apply to the consumption of natural resources. Concern was expressed about reliance on the use of trade measures to enforce MEAs (see Section 3.4); it was felt that so-called 'positive measures' (financial support and technology transfer) were at least as important, and probably more so, for developing countries. The importance of effective compliance mechanisms for MEAs was, however, recognized; while in an ideal world, trade measures might be undesirable, it was acknowledged that in practice there were not often many alternatives.

Chapter 4

Resolving Trade and Environment Disputes

4.1 Introduction
Juan Carlos Sanchez Arnau

Let me start by defining the issues to be discussed in this session and describing the present situation of the debate in the WTO.

1. Trade measures have been included in a relatively small number of MEAs (less than 20 out of a total of approximately 200 MEAs identified by the WTO Secretariat). These measures are of different natures and play different roles in the context of each MEA. Therefore it is very difficult to make general judgments about their compliance with WTO requirements.
2. Up to now there has been no GATT or WTO dispute on measures applied pursuant to an MEA. In other words, no conflict has emerged between WTO rules and MEA rules.
3. At the same time, there is an increasing number of WTO disputes arising from the application of national trade measures based on environmental concerns. The large majority of these disputes originate in the extra-jurisdictionality of the environmental legislation of one country.
4. Almost all MEAs include provisions to increase transparency through the collection and exchange of information, the coordination of technical and scientific research and the collective monitoring of implementing measures as well as through consultation provisions. They also contain mechanisms for resolving disputes. These range from non-binding consensus-building mechanisms to binding judicial procedures of arbitration, and, for some of the MEAs, resort to the International Court of Justice.

5. The analysis made by the WTO Committee on Trade and Environment (CTE) of the dispute settlement mechanisms found in MEAs showed that there was no incompatibility between the solution of disputes arising in the framework of a MEA and the dispute settlement mechanism established by the WTO.

6. Three different kinds of dispute were analysed by the CTE:

    (a) Disputes between two WTO members, parties to a MEA, over the use of trade measures they are applying between themselves pursuant to the MEA. In this case the CTE noted that: 'They should consider trying to resolve the problem through the dispute settlement mechanisms available under the MEA.'[74] Moreover, the CTE also noted that: 'In practice, in cases where there is a consensus among parties to a MEA to apply among themselves specifically mandated trade measures. disputes between them over the use of such measures are unlikely to occur in the WTO.'[75]

    (b) Disputes arising between a WTO member that is party to a MEA and one that is not party to the MEA as a consequence of trade measures applied by the former, following their obligations under the MEA. In this case the CTE was unable to find a procedure that would avoid the eventual conflict of laws. However, it stressed that: 'In the negotiation of a future MEA, particular care should be taken over how trade measures may be considered for application to non-parties.'[76] At the same time, the CTE report does not limit the possibility for any WTO member to resort to WTO dispute mechanisms if it considers that its rights are affected by actions taken by other member parties over the use of trade measures taken pursuant to the MEA.

    (c) The case of unilateral measures based on environmental considerations adopted by a WTO member against another WTO member. In this case the CTE agreed that: 'Most of the delegations which intervened in the debate on this issue stated that they consider that the provisions of GATT Article XX do not permit a Member to

---

[74] *Report of the Committee on Trade and Environment* (WTO, 1996), para. 178.

[75] Ibid., para. 174.

[76] Ibid.

impose unilateral trade restrictions that are otherwise inconsistent with its WTO obligations for the purpose of protecting environmental resources that lie outside its jurisdiction. For them, a renewed commitment needs to be taken by WTO Members to avoid using trade measures unilaterally for that purpose, and numerous proposals have been made in the CTE to that effect. Another view is that there is nothing in the text of Article XX which indicates that it only applies to policies to protect animal or plant resources or conserve natural resources within the territory of the country invoking the provision. A number of Members noted that there were differing views as to what constituted unilateralism.'[77] The CTE also endorsed Principle 12 of the Rio Declaration and stressed that there is a clear complementarity between the approach of this principle and the work of the WTO in seeking cooperative multilateral solutions to trade concerns.

7. Finally, after analysing the functioning of the WTO dispute settlement provisions and the request for wider participation of environmental experts in such mechanism, the CTE recognized 'the benefit of having all relevant expertise available to the WTO panels in cases involving treaty related environmental measures, including trade measures taken pursuant to MEAs'.[78] Moreover, the CTE stressed that the provisions of the Dispute Settlement Understanding (DSU) 'provide the means for a panel to seek information and technical advice from any individual or body which it deems appropriate and to consult experts, including by establishing expert review groups'.[79]

8. Despite these clarifications, which I believe will inspire decisions to be taken by future panels, the CTE will continue working towards the clarification of pending matters, such as relations between parties and non-parties to an MEA. Some valuable proposals have been submitted for the Committee's consideration or in the context of informal negotiations. However, the major difficulty lies in the different perceptions of the nature of a potential conflict between trade measures and

---

[77] Ibid., para. 8.
[78] Ibid., para 179.
[79] Ibid.

environmental objectives – conflict which the reality has not shown up to now. Conflicts have essentially arisen in the case of unilateral measures of extra-jurisdictional nature, and in these cases the GATT and WTO mechanism for dispute settlement has shown and continues to show its efficiency.

I mentioned in my initial comments the existence of a number of proposals to deal with potential conflicts between trade measures taken pursuant to MEAs and WTO rules. Let me mention three that I believe could help to advance matters in this field.

One of these would be to agree that 'Disputes brought to the Dispute Settlement Mechanism (DSM) of the WTO should be resolved on a case-by-case basis'. Nevertheless, consideration of disputes should be informed by the following recommendations:

- If the dispute arises between a party and a non-party to an MEA, and the trade measure could be considered to have been taken pursuant to an MEA, there should be a refutable presumption (*iuris tantum*) that the measure is consistent with the multilateral trading system.
- On the contrary, if the trade measure at issue is unilaterally inspired and addresses an environmental externality that impacts strictly beyond the boundary of the WTO member that takes the measure, there should be a *iuris tantum* that the measure is inconsistent with the multilateral trading system.

Another proposal would be to make explicitly applicable some general principles of law of the multilateral trading system. One of these principles states that customary rules of interpretation of public international law could be applied in order to clarify provisions of agreements covered by the multilateral trading system. Of particular relevance among these rules is Article 30 of the Vienna Convention on the Interpretation of Treaties, which states: 'When all parties to the earlier treaty are parties also to the later treaty (but the earlier treaty is not terminated or suspended in operation under Article 59), the earlier treaty applies only to the extent that its provisions are compatible with those of the later treaty.'

The above-mentioned principles, which most probably will inform eventual decisions to be taken by panels, would permit clarification of the relations between two WTO members that become parties to a MEA. With these principles in place, there would be little room for confusion between the rights and obligations of WTO members in connection with their positions as parties to an MEA.

The third proposal which if adopted could improve the DSM is the following: 'The co-operative agreement concluded between the WTO and IMF could serve, to some extent, as a basis for the institutional relationship between the WTO and MEAs. This would provide the opportunity for concerned MEAs (in line with paragraph 6 of the WTO/IMF agreement) to attend as observers to the meetings of the Dispute Settlement Body where matters relevant to the given MEA are considered, and also to submit its views to a panel on any trade measure relevant to the MEA at issue, following the same procedure to be established by the General Council for IMF submissions.'

4.2 Lessons from the European experience[80]
Damien Geradin

The interface between trade and environmental protection raises several concerns which vary depending on the type of environmental measure in question. In this regard, a distinction must be drawn between:

(a) direct restrictions on trade;
(b) product standards;
(c) process standards.

---

[80] For further explorations of this issue, see: Damien Geradin, *Trade and the Environment: A Comparative Study of EC and US Law* (Cambridge: Cambridge University Press, 1997); Damien Geradin, 'Trade and Environmental Protection: Community Harmonization and National Environmental Standards', in A. Barav and D. Wyatt, eds, *Yearbook of European Law*, Vol. 13 (Oxford: Oxford University Press, 1994), p. 152; and Damien Geradin, 'Free Trade and Environmental Protection in an Integrated Market – A Survey of the Case-Law of the United States Supreme Court and the European Court of Justice', *Journal of Transnational Law and Policy*, 2 (1993), p. 141.

Direct restrictions on trade

Trade and environmental protection disputes arise when member states impose direct restrictions on the imports or exports of goods in order to pursue environmental goals. To protect their environment, member states may, for example, ban the imports of waste into their territory or ban exports of endangered species of fauna or flora.

Product standards

Although they do not directly regulate intra-Community trade, product standards (i.e. standards regulating the characteristics of products) may have restrictive effects on trade. First, product standards may be used as an instrument of protectionism when their effect is to discriminate between domestic and non-domestic products. In addition, in the absence of a discriminatory effect, inconsistent product standards impede intra-Community trade by denying manufacturers the ability to realize economies of scale in production and distribution and by generally creating market fragmentation.

Process standards

Process standards (i.e. standards regulating the production methods used by manufacturers) may raise several trade and environment concerns. First, differences in the stringency of process standards among member states distort competition. Producers located in member states enforcing strict process standards will suffer a competitive disadvantage compared with producers located in member states enforcing less strict standards. All things being equal, this may result in increased sales, market share and profitability for those producers located in low-standard member states.

Second, though this is supported by little empirical evidence, differences in the level of stringency of process standards may induce industrial relocation as cost-cutting producers seek out low-standard jurisdictions.

Finally, faced with the prospect of their industries suffering a competitive disadvantage when compared with companies located in low-standard jurisdictions, member states may choose not to elevate environmental standards or may even relax current standards. This may trigger a 'race to the bottom', i.e. a 'race from the desirable levels of environmental protection that member states would pursue if they did not face competition to the increasingly undesirable levels they choose in the face of such competition'.[81]

The responses

In the EC, the concerns raised by the interface between trade and environmental policies can essentially be dealt with through two complementary institutional responses: selective invalidation of trade-restrictive environmental standards; and harmonization of environmental standards by the EC.

First, the European Court of Justice (ECJ) can use the free trade provisions of the EC Treaty (Articles 30 et seq.) to place limits on the ability of member states to adopt trade-restrictive environmental legislation. Alternatively, the EC can set common environmental standards for all member states in order to avoid the trade distortions that may be generated by inconsistent member-state regulations. The rest of this paper will focus on the first of these responses.

The trade and environment case law of the European Court of Justice

First we have a brief overview of the main trade and environment cases dealt with by the ECJ.

Case 1: Danish Bottles

In this case, the ECJ examined the compatibility with the EC Treaty of Danish legislation requiring drinks manufacturers: (1) to set up a deposit-and-return system for the containers they place on the Danish market; and (2) to have such containers approved by the National Agency for the Pro-

---

[81] See Richard Revesz, 'Rehabilitating Interstate Competition: Rethinking the "Race-to-the-Bottom" Rationale for Federal Environmental Regulation', *New York University Law Review*, 67 (1992), p. 1210.

tection of the Environment (NAPE). The ECJ admitted the compatibility of the deposit-and-return system with the EC Treaty on the ground that it was a proportionate means of achieving a legitimate environmental objective (i.e., to keep streets clean of bottles). By contrast, the ECJ considered that the NAPE approval system was incompatible with the EC Treaty because it was disproportionate.

Case 2: Belgian Waste

In this case, the ECJ was asked to examine the compatibility with the EC Treaty of a Decree of the Belgian region of Wallonia imposing a ban on the imports of all waste products into its territory. The ECJ ruled that, in so far as it concerned non-dangerous waste, such a ban was compatible with the EC Treaty because it aimed at achieving a legitimate environmental objective. To support its judgment, the ECJ expressly referred to the principle of correction of environmental harm at source enunciated in Article 130R(2) of the EC Treaty and the principles of proximity and self-sufficiency contained in the Basel Convention on the Control of Transboundary Movements of Hazardous Waste.

Case 3: Crayfish

Here, the ECJ was asked by the Commission to declare incompatible with the EC Treaty a German ban on the imports of live European freshwater crayfish. Though the ECJ recognized that the German ban was pursuing a legitimate environmental objective (i.e. to protect domestic crayfish against disease), it considered that this ban was disproportionate. The German government could have achieved the same environmental objectives by using less trade-restrictive measures.

A number of general conclusions can be drawn from the above cases.

- The ECJ has admitted that there are circumstances in which environmental objectives must be given precedence to free trade (see *Danish Bottles* and *Belgian Waste* cases).
- In its trade and environment case-law, the ECJ has taken into account

well recognized environmental principles, such as the principle of correction of environmental damage at source contained in Article 130R(2) or other principles contained in multilateral environmental agreements (see *Belgian Waste* case).

- The ECJ has not accepted that any type of environmental measure should be seen as legitimate under the EC Treaty. In particular, the ECJ has generally applied a strict test of proportionality to trade-restrictive environmental measures (see *Danish Bottles* and *Crayfish* cases).

- The ECJ has had to deal with relatively few trade and environment cases. Moreover, unlike GATT dispute settlement panels, it has never had to deal with the most difficult type of trade and environment cases, namely those dealing with process standards. The reason for this is that the EC has widely harmonized product and process standards. Such a harmonization process, which has been extremely flexible, has enabled the avoidance of many trade and environment problems.

What can the WTO learn from the EC experience?

Unlike the WTO, the ECJ has recognized the importance of environmental protection as a policy objective. When dealing with trade and environment disputes, the ECJ has also taken into account environmental principles, such as the principles contained in Article 130R(2) of the Treaty, as well as in multilateral environmental agreements. Such an approach could provide a useful reference for the WTO.

More fundamentally, it seems that, with respect to trade and environment, the great advantage of the EC is its ability to harmonize environmental product standards and process standards. Harmonization of environmental standards both facilitates the avoidance of trade and environment disputes, and enables a correct balance to be struck between trade and environmental protection. It is therefore suggested that, in the future, a central challenge for the WTO (or other international body) will be to develop strategies to harmonize, or at least coordinate, national environmental policies.

Discussion

The main point brought out in the discussion following this paper was the precise role and powers of the ECJ. It was generally agreed that the Court's powers did not, and should not, extend to judging the validity of the environmental objectives of the measures in question, but that they could legitimately deal with the necessity and proportionality of the measures. A cautionary note was sounded, however: this is in itself a highly controversial decision, and could lead the Court into making decisions on the desirability of alternatives to the measures under challenge without actually having much knowledge, or seeking any evidence, on their efficacy. It was also noted that the case law of the ECJ in this area was not always especially clear, and that it was difficult to derive general guidelines from it for policy-makers considering alternative courses of action.

A secondary issue was the desirability of harmonization of policies; the point was made by participants in the discussion that in the area of animal welfare, for example, the Commission was increasingly shying away from implementing relatively high EC standards (such as the ban on fur caught in leghold traps) because of the anticipated responses of the EU's major trading partners, and the fear of a challenge under the WTO. While noting that animal welfare was a difficult area for this debate, because of the absence of physical spillover effects (unlike, for example, transboundary pollution), Dr Geradin pointed out that the EU had been highly innovative and flexible in its pursuit of harmonization, and the difficulties were perhaps less than often believed.[82] One example was the 'bubble' for greenhouse gas emissions, where the overall EU target for emission reductions was comprised of widely varying individual targets for member states.

---

[82] See Daniel C. Esty and Damien Geradin, 'Market Access, Competitiveness and Harmonization: Dealing with Trade and Environmental Protection in the European Community and NAFTA', *Harvard Environmental Law Review*, 21 (1997), p. 265.

4.3 WTO dispute settlement: the environmental dimension
Jeffrey L. Gertler [83]

The Parties to this Agreement, ... allowing for the optimal use of the world's resources in accordance with the objective of sustainable development, seeking both to protect and preserve the environment and to enhance the means for doing so in a manner consistent with their respective needs and concerns at different levels of economic development, ... Agree as follows: ...

(from Preamble to Marrakesh Agreement Establishing
the World Trade Organization)

The GATT, which entered into force (provisionally) in 1948 and celebrates its fiftieth anniversary in 1998 (although it is now just one of many agreements annexed to the WTO Agreement), did not refer explicitly to such concepts as the protection of the environment or sustainable development. And yet, the dispute settlement procedures of this trade treaty have been used more frequently to resolve intergovernmental disputes over trade-related environmental measures (TREMs) than those of any other dispute settlement system. From 1982 to 1995, seven such disputes were resolved through GATT dispute panels.

This 'trend', if we can call it that, has continued under its successor, the WTO Agreement, which entered into force in January 1995. So far the WTO dispute settlement system has been used to adjudicate three disputes involving TREMs and there are several more on the front burner. Also, in contrast to the GATT, the WTO Agreement does explicitly refer to environmental protection and sustainable development. Furthermore, of all the different trade-related topics proposed at the end of the Uruguay Round for examination by the newly created WTO (including the linkage of trade with the environment, internationally recognized labour standards, competition policy, foreign investment, immigration policies, debt and alleviation of poverty), only the linkage between trade and environment was given the green light through the creation of the WTO Committee on Trade and Environment.

[83] The views expressed in this paper are those of the author and should not be attributed to the WTO. The paper draws upon work by Richard Eglin, Robert Hudec, Additya Mattoo, Petros Mavroidis, Ernst-Ulrich Petersmann, Frieder Roessler, David Runnals, Sabrina Shaw and Brennan Van Dyke.

This paper attempts to summarize the basic WTO principles as they relate to TREMs, to highlight the evolution of GATT/WTO dispute settlement procedures and the application of these procedures to disputes involving TREMs, and to touch on problem areas that could benefit from further examination.

WTO principles as they relate to TREMs

Most national and international environmental policies can be implemented through measures consistent with the rules of the multilateral trading system as set out in the WTO Agreement. These rules exist mainly to ensure non-discrimination and security and predictability in conditions of trade.

The WTO's non-discrimination rules are of two main types. The first is embodied in Article I of the GATT and is known as the 'most-favoured nation' (or 'MFN') clause, according to which WTO members are bound to grant to the products of other members treatment no less favourable than that accorded to the products of any other country. Thus, no member is to give special trading advantages to another or to discriminate against it; all are on an equal basis and all share the benefits of any moves towards lower trade barriers. A second form of non-discrimination, known as 'national treatment', requires that once goods have entered a national market they be treated no less favourably than like domestically produced goods. This provision is contained in GATT Article III. Similar MFN and national treatment principles are embodied in the WTO's Agreement on Trade in Services (GATS) and in the Agreement on Trade-Related Aspects of Intellectual Property Rights (TRIPS).

Security and predictability in the multilateral trading system are determined largely through the WTO requirements that border protection be achieved (and reduced over time) through import tariffs rather than quotas or other less transparent non-tariff measures, and that member governments publish and notify all their measures that impact on trade in goods, services and intellectual property rights.

All of the above disciplines and many others (the WTO Agreement contains some 29 individual legal texts covering everything from agriculture and textiles to trade-related investment measures, and 25 additional ministerial declarations) are bound together through an integrated system of dispute settlement. Out of this system has evolved a reasonably coherent set of interpretations of multilateral trade disciplines and a highly developed legal order in the area of international economic affairs.

The operation of the WTO's non-discrimination and transparency rules allow for very wide scope in the choice of instruments to achieve national and multilateral environmental policies. With regard to domestic environmental policies, the main limitation is that the policies (and in particular the instruments used to implement such policies) must in principle not discriminate between foreign sources of like products (Article I, MFN) or in favour of domestic like products on the internal market (Article III, national treatment). And members may derogate from these two non-discrimination principles where necessary, but only in circumstances where less trade-restrictive measures consistent with the WTO are not reasonably available. These exceptions are provided in, *inter alia*, GATT Article XX(b) ('measures necessary to protect human, animal or plant life or health') and Article XX(g) ('measures relating to the conservation of exhaustible natural resources if such measures are made effective in conjunction with restrictions on domestic production or consumption').

Despite these exceptions, allowing governments to use more trade-restrictive measures to achieve their environmental policy goals, there is in general little need for WTO members to resort to such measures. This is because, as is taught by the theory of optimal intervention (which ranks various instruments according to the economic efficiency with which they attain policy goals), the optimal instrument is the one that attains the policy with the fewest undesired side-effects, usually the one that attacks the identified policy problem directly at its source. In contrast, a measure discriminating between goods and services according to their origin (or destination) is rarely an optimal measure with which to attain a domestic policy goal, including in the area of the environment, and such measures are generally not consistent with WTO rules. In WTO terms, the more direct policy instruments are border tax adjustments, domestic subsidies, non-discriminatory taxes and import and export tariffs (all WTO-legal forms of intervention), whereas the less direct, less transparent instruments are quotas and other non-tariff measures and regulations discriminating against imported products (both in principle not WTO-consistent).

As an illustration, take a member government's domestic policy objective of reducing pollution emitted from automobiles. Direct forms of intervention, entirely consistent with WTO rules, would be to require lower exhaust emissions from all cars on its territory, both imported and domestic; to impose a heavy tax on (or ban altogether) dirtier forms of gasoline or car engines; or to subsidize – through tax breaks or other financial or regulatory measures – cleaner gasoline or automotive production or consumption. Less direct and discriminatory forms of intervention, such as imposing a higher pollution tax only on imported cars, would not be WTO-consistent and equally would be less efficient in achieving the member's policy objective.

It should be noted that the WTO has tightened the discipline applicable to the choice of policy instruments in a number of areas of domestic policy regulations, that is, regulations that are equally applicable to domestic and foreign goods, services and service suppliers. Particularly in respect of technical regulations and sanitary and phytosanitary measures, unlike under the GATT, it is no longer sufficient to show that domestic measures are non-discriminatory, in other words that they accord national treatment to imported products. The WTO Agreement on Technical Barriers to Trade (TBT Agreement) obliges members to 'ensure that technical regulations are not prepared, adopted or applied with a view to or with the effect of creating unnecessary obstacles to international trade. For this purpose, technical regulations shall not be more trade-restrictive than necessary to fulfil a legitimate objective ...' (Article 2.2). And the Agreement on Sanitary and Phytosanitary Measures (SPS Agreement) requires members to base their sanitary and phytosanitary measures on science and risk assessment (Articles 5.1 and 5.2) and to ensure that these measures are not 'more trade-restrictive than required to achieve their appropriate level of sanitary or phytosanitary protection ...' (Article 5.6). It can safely be said, however, that the objective of both the TBT and SPS Agreements is not to prevent the legitimate exercise of domestic regulatory authority, but to forestall protectionism in the guise of technical regulations and SPS measures.

The situation gets somewhat more complicated as one moves from domestic environmental policy objectives to efforts by member governments to achieve external environmental policy objectives elsewhere in the world, either in transboundary situations or in the international commons or within the territory of another member. Generally, one can distinguish three different types of dispute between WTO members, requiring three different lines of legal analysis:

1. disputes where the TREM is authorized under a multilateral environmental agreement (MEA) to which both WTO members subscribe;
2. disputes where only the WTO member taking the TREM is signatory to the MEA;
3. disputes where the WTO member taking the TREM acts unilaterally without the cover of any MEA.

In the first case, in disputes between WTO members over the WTO consistency of TREMs based on MEAs accepted by both parties to the dispute, it could be argued that the members may waive their rights and obligations under the WTO Agreement to the extent of any inconsistency with MEA-authorized TREMs. Depending on the intentions of the parties, such an interpretation could be consistent with Articles 30 and 41 of the Vienna Convention on the Law of Treaties, which provide for modification of treaty terms as between the parties through subsequently concluded treaties. A WTO dispute panel would be likely to take into account as necessary modifications to the interpretation of WTO rules resulting from a MEA to which both WTO members were signatories. Also, depending on the dispute settlement provisions of the MEA, the parties to the MEA might choose to resolve their dispute within the forum provided under the MEA.

The analysis becomes more difficult as one moves to the second case, where disputes arise between WTO members over the WTO consistency of TREMs provided for in MEAs accepted by only one party to the dispute. Clearly, and in line with Article 30 of the Vienna Convention on the Law of Treaties, without the agreement of the non-MEA party or some 'creative' interpretation by the WTO of the necessity test under Article XX(b) of the GATT, a WTO member may not claim legal cover for a TREM under a MEA to which the other WTO member is not a signatory.

It is noteworthy that WTO members within the WTO Committee on Trade and Environment, as well as other international governmental and non-governmental organizations in other fora, have devoted considerable attention and energies to resolving potential conflicts in this area. Various proposals have been made as to ways in which the WTO might accommodate MEA-authorized TREMs, particularly where the MEAs have sufficiently universal membership and the environmental harms are sufficiently important. Many of these proposals revolve around the possibility of interpreting the necessity test of GATT Article XX(b) to cover discriminatory actions taken under MEAs against non-signatories. Members are also considering proposals to amend Article XX to provide for an exception covering discriminatory provisions in MEAs similar to the exception covering commodity agreements in Article XX(h). Yet another possibility is a waiver of the MFN clause in GATT Article I to cover TREMs under MEAs that discriminate against non-signatories. This would require three-quarters of WTO members to vote in favour of the waiver. Suffice it to say at this juncture that we can anticipate more and further refinement of proposals in this area and the eventual elaboration of improved accommodation of multilateral environmental concerns in the WTO.

Finally, in the third case, where there is a dispute between WTO members over the unilateral imposition of a TREM, without even the pretence of cover of an MEA, WTO law is clear in condemning such unilateral action to the extent that it is discriminatory (i.e. denies MFN and/or national treatment) or is not covered by one of the enumerated exceptions to MFN and national treatment found in GATT Article XX. The WTO Understanding on the Rules and Procedures Governing the Settlement of Disputes ('Dispute Settlement Understanding', DSU) also provides that, in seeking redress of WTO violations or nullification of benefits, WTO members shall have recourse exclusively to the dispute settlement rules and procedures of the DSU and shall not make unilateral determinations of claimed violations or nullification of benefits (DSU Article 23).

The WTO dispute settlement system

From 1948, the GATT regulated the settlement of disputes among member countries principally through its Articles XXII and XXIII. These provisions ensured the right of consultations on matters in dispute between individual members and, where such consultations did not result in a mutually satis-factory solution, mandated the GATT Contracting Parties (the collective body of GATT members) to examine the matter, issue rulings or recom-mendations as appropriate, and authorize retaliatory suspension of con-cessions if circumstances were serious enough to warrant such action. Thus, the primary emphasis was placed on consultations aimed at finding a mutually satisfactory solution to matters in dispute. But where consult-ations were not successful, resort could be had to more formal dispute resolution procedures aimed at protecting the rights of all member governments.

The scope of GATT Article XXIII was very broad: the dispute could involve nullification or impairment of a benefit accruing under the GATT either as the result of a measure alleged to be inconsistent with the GATT ('violation complaint'), or of a measure not alleged to be inconsistent ('non-violation complaint'), or even as the result of 'any other situation'. However, the vast majority of complaints have concerned measures alleged to be in violation of the GATT.

The procedures for the establishment and functioning of dispute settlement panels evolved over several decades and were first codified in an Understanding at the conclusion of the Tokyo Round of multilateral trade negotiations in 1979. Further codification of practice occurred in 1982, 1984 and 1989. Decisions on the establishment of GATT panels were in principle subject to simple majority vote but in practice were always taken by consensus. This consensus-based decision-making instilled confidence but resulted at times in temporary blocking of the process by the member government subject to a complaint. The composition of the panel and its terms of reference were also subject to agreement by the parties to the dispute, resulting in two further points in the process where the defending party could seek to block or delay dispute resolution. And yet, among the 126 panels established between 1948 and 1994, the overwhelming majority proceeded through the examination stage and issued reports containing findings and recommendations within a very reasonable period of time, averaging seven months in the later years.

Once constituted, panels would request written submissions from the complaining and responding parties, hold at least two substantive meetings with the parties, and give interested third parties an opportunity to present their views. The panel would then proceed, assisted by Secretariat staff, to draft its report and submit it to the GATT Council (the executive body of GATT members, potentially comprising the entire membership). The panel's findings and recommendations would have legally binding effect only once the panel report was adopted by the GATT Council. These decisions on adoption were also subject to consensus, providing a sort of political check to the quasi-judicial panel process, but also providing an opportunity for disputing parties to forestall completion of formal dispute resolution. Fortunately, although the 'losing' party often succeeded in blocking adoption of a panel report during successive GATT Council meetings, such blockages seldom extended beyond a few months, and there have been only very few instances of a report being blocked indefinitely. In contrast to this experience in the GATT, the record on adoption was far less propitious for panel reports issued under the separately negotiated Tokyo Round Anti-Dumping and Subsidies Codes, each of which had its own dispute settlement procedures.

The typical recommendation of a panel in a case where a party's measure was found to be inconsistent with the GATT would be for the party concerned to bring its measure into conformity with its obligations. Where the finding was one of nullification or impairment resulting from a non-violation (for instance, the impairment of a tariff concession resulting from the introduction of an unforeseen but perfectly legal domestic production subsidy), the party concerned would be directed to consider ways and means of making a satisfactory adjustment, but would not be required to remove the measure in issue. If the panel's findings and recommendations were adverse to the party complained against, that party would have a reasonable period of time to come into compliance with the panel's recommendations following the Council's adoption of the panel report. No precise guidelines were developed as to what constituted a 'reasonable' period of time, but it was generally understood that the time frame would necessarily vary depending upon the nature of the measure and whether action by the legislative branch of government, in addition to the executive branch, would be required to bring an inconsistent measure into conformity with the GATT.

The party charged with implementing a recommendation would be encouraged, pending full implementation, to negotiate temporary compensation. But because such compensation would by definition be voluntary in nature, the only real weapon available to the winning party to ensure full compliance with an adopted panel recommendation (other than that of pressure from trading partners) would be to obtain authorization from the GATT Council to retaliate temporarily through the suspension of concessions towards the party delaying implementation beyond a reasonable period of time. Here again, however, the decision to authorize retaliation would be taken by consensus, and such authorization was granted only once in the history of the GATT: in 1952, against the United States and in favour of the Netherlands. Even in that case, despite authorization from the Council, the Netherlands did not take retaliatory action. The generalized non-use of retaliation since the GATT's earliest days would seem to suggest that the peer pressure of trading partners was largely effective in ensuring compliance with dispute settlement rulings and recommendations.

Over the four and a half decades since its modest beginnings, a number of problems surfaced in the day-to-day operation of the GATT dispute settlement system. Many of these were addressed and resolved through the Uruguay Round negotiations.

Foremost among these was the concern over the fragmented approach to dispute settlement resulting from multiple treaties having overlapping jurisdictions dealing with related trade matters. Contracting parties of the GATT 1947, which were also signatories to various of the Tokyo Round Codes (negotiated under GATT auspices and concluded in 1979), had the option of seeking the most advantageous among the various dispute settlement procedures of seven of these Codes ('forum shopping'). This state of affairs led to conflicts (both real and potential) in respect of panel establishment, re-litigation in a second forum of issues already argued and decided in another, and inconsistent results putting member governments in the untenable position of being subject to inconsistent obligations.

Particularly troublesome were the overlapping jurisdictions of the GATT with the Subsidies Code and the Civil Aircraft Code.

Reflecting many years of negotiation and eleventh-hour compromise, the WTO's Dispute Settlement Understanding resolves this problem of fragmentation by creating an integrated system of dispute settlement covering all the Agreements concluded under the Uruguay Round. The system is managed under a single authority, the Dispute Settlement Body (DSB). The DSB has the sole authority to establish panels, adopt panel and appellate reports, maintain surveillance of implementation of rulings and recommendations, and authorize retaliatory measures in cases of non-implementation.

Also very high on the agenda of problems addressed in the Uruguay Round was the concern over delays and undue political interference engendered by the practice of requiring consensus-based decision-making at all stages of formal dispute resolution. As summarized above, consensus decisions were required for the establishment of panels, adoption of panel reports and authorization to retaliate. In addition, the composition and terms of reference of panels were subject to the agreement of the parties to the dispute. At each of these decision stages parties had the opportunity to block movement to the next stage. The response of negotiators in the Uruguay Round was to focus on ways of injecting greater automaticity into the process, the result being a greatly streamlined procedure, including virtually automatic decisions within specified time frames throughout the dispute settlement process.

As early as May 1989, following improvements agreed at the Mid-Term Review of the Uruguay Round, held in Montreal in December 1988 and put into force by the GATT on a trial basis, dispute settlement became subject to greater automaticity in decisions on the establishment, terms of reference and composition of panels, such that these decisions were no longer dependent upon the consent of the parties to a dispute. These reforms are carried over into the WTO. If, after 60 days of a request for consultations, there is no settlement, the complaining party may proceed to request the establishment of a panel. The DSU requires the establishment of a panel no later than at the meeting of the DSB following that at which a request is made, unless the DSB decides by consensus against such establishment. Thus, the consensus rule has been reversed: rather than affirmative consensus being required to establish a panel, henceforth negative consensus (a very unlikely occurrence, given the complaining party's desire for a panel) is required to prevent establishment.

Also carried over from the Mid-Term Review improvements, the DSU provides specific rules and deadlines for deciding the terms of reference and composition of panels. Standard terms of reference apply unless the parties agree to special terms within 20 days of the panel's establishment. And, where the parties do not agree on the composition of the panel within the same 20 days, this can be referred to the Director-General of the WTO who must decide on the panel's composition within ten days. Whether they be government officials or not, panellists must serve in their individual capacities, must not accept instructions from their governments, and in principle may not be from countries having an interest in the dispute.

Uruguay Round negotiators significantly extended the automatic nature of dispute resolution in the WTO by providing that within 60 days of their issuance panel reports shall be adopted, unless the DSB decides by consensus not to adopt the report (the same negative consensus rule as above) or one of the parties notifies the DSB of its decision to appeal. Thus, virtually automatic adoption of panel reports is tempered by the creation of a new appellate review procedure. A standing Appellate Body is established, composed of seven members, three of whom are to serve on any one case. An appeal is to be limited to issues of law covered in the panel report and legal interpretations developed by the panel. Appellate proceedings should not exceed 60 days but in any case may not exceed 90 days from the date a party formally notifies its decision to appeal. The resulting report is also subject to quasi-automatic adoption: it is to be adopted by the DSB and unconditionally accepted by the parties within 30 days following its issuance to members, unless the DSB decides by consensus against its adoption. In these early days of the WTO it is difficult to forecast how often members will resort to the new appellate procedures. But so far, all five panel reports issued since the entry into force of the WTO Agreement have been the subject of appeal.

Further automaticity has been introduced into the dispute settlement process at the implementation stage. Once the panel report and the

Appellate Body report are adopted, the party concerned must notify its intentions with respect to implementation of adopted recommendations. If it is impracticable to comply immediately, the party shall be given a reasonable period of time, the latter to be decided either by agreement of the parties and approval by the DSB within 45 days of adoption of the report or through arbitration within 90 days of adoption. In any event, the DSB is to keep the implementation under regular surveillance until the issue is resolved. Within a specified time frame, parties are to enter into negotiations to agree on mutually acceptable compensation. However, where this has not been agreed, a party to the dispute may request authorization of the DSB to suspend concessions or other obligations to the other party concerned. The DSB is to grant such authorization within 30 days of the expiry of the agreed time frame for implementation, again unless the DSB decides by consensus to reject the request. Disagreements over the proposed level of suspension may be referred to arbitration. In principle, this retaliation is to occur in the same sector as that at issue in the panel case. But where this would not be practicable or effective, the concept of cross-retaliation is introduced whereby the party may suspend concessions in a different sector of the same agreement or, in exceptional circumstances, under an entirely different agreement.

This combination of virtually automatic approval with the possibility of cross-retaliating in different sectors or under different agreements may well lead WTO members to go beyond threats of retaliation to actually take such action in response to delayed compliance with adopted panel and appellate body recommendations. And yet, a possibly troublesome aspect of the DSU's provisions is that they require the level of such retaliation to be 'equivalent to' the level of nullification or impairment. The drafters of GATT Article XXIII clearly intended retaliatory suspension of concessions as a temporary remedy, pending action by the party concerned to bring its measure into conformity with treaty obligations. In contrast, this new equivalency (or reciprocity) principle as applied to retaliation may have the unfortunate effect of limiting the incentive for the party concerned to do away with the inconsistency.

In many respects, however, the integrated nature of dispute settlement in the WTO, the greater automaticity in decision-making and the tighter time frames for completion of procedures under the DSU should reduce the potential (and the incentive) for unilateral action by WTO members, making it far less likely that members will seek to take matters into their own hands. Indeed, while unilateral action in disputes relating to trade matters covered by the WTO is expressly outlawed by the DSU, it can be argued that the new system's greater automaticity and tighter time frames effectively ensure the multilateralization of salient features of certain domestic procedures.

One area where it can be convincingly argued that further change in the system is required is in respect of transparency. While confidentiality has been a hallmark of both GATT and WTO dispute settlement proceedings, the legitimacy of the decisions taken pursuant to the WTO dispute settlement system depend increasingly on the legitimacy of the dispute settlement procedures that lead to these decisions. As a result, more openness and transparency in the procedures become essential elements in achieving legitimacy and public acceptability of WTO dispute settlement decisions. The challenge will be to arrive at the right balance of openness that will instil greater confidence and legitimacy in the process without undermining the effectiveness of the multilateral trade policy machinery.

The jury is still out as to the overall effectiveness of the new dispute settlement procedures of the WTO. Whereas the system to date has evolved gradually and has been progressively codified as customary practice, the Uruguay Round results in this area are a dramatic departure from this evolutionary process. GATT dispute settlement always reflected a tension between diplomatic, negotiated solutions on the one hand, and legal, rule-based decision-making on the other, with the two approaches vying for dominance at different times over the history of this institution. Certainly, the rule-based, more judicial or legalistic approach has had the upper hand in the last 15 years and will undoubtedly be given a further shot in the arm by the detailed and significantly strengthened rules of the Dispute Settlement Understanding. But, because of this long-standing tension between the two approaches, there is likely to be continued demand and continued need for flexibility somewhere within the system. If there is less 'give' in the dispute settlement procedures, one could reasonably expect greater recourse by WTO members to safeguard actions, the renegotiation of market access concessions and requests for waivers from WTO obligations.

Overall, and despite the uncertainties inherent in the implementation of the newly strengthened rules and procedures, the integrated dispute settlement system of the WTO is proving to be a central element in providing security and predictability to the multilateral trading system. It is to be expected that the greater certainty in interpretation of principles and provisions of the WTO Agreements resulting from application of the WTO dispute settlement system over time will lead to the coherent expansion of GATT/WTO jurisprudence to the benefit of governments, traders, producers, consumers and all those affected by international trade in their daily activities.

Review of GATT/WTO panels involving TREMs

As noted at the outset, seven panel cases involving TREMs have been adjudicated under GATT and three under the WTO Agreement. Several more are in the pipeline. Probably the most noteworthy observation one can make in regard to these cases (quite aside from their sheer number) is that none of them scrutinizes or even so much as questions the underlying environmental objectives or policies of the member governments concerned; the dispute settlement panels focus their attention entirely and exclusively on the instruments (or measures) used to achieve these environmental policies. Another relevant observation is that to date none of the cases adjudicated has involved the interplay of GATT/WTO law and an MEA.

The first case involving a TREM was a 1982 panel dealing with a Canadian complaint against a US prohibition on imports of tuna. The import prohibition was introduced as a counter-measure under the US Fishery Conservation and Management Act following the seizure of 19 fishing vessels and the arrest by Canadian authorities of a number of US fishermen fishing for albacore tuna within 200 miles of the west coast of Canada, without authorization from the Canadian government, in waters regarded by Canada as being under its fisheries jurisdiction. The United States did not recognize the Canadian claim to jurisdiction over tuna in these waters and retaliated pursuant to its Fisheries Act. The panel concluded that the US import prohibition was inconsistent with GATT Article XI:1 and was not justified under Article XI:2 or Article XX(g). In particular, the panel found that the US prohibition had not been 'made effective in conjunction with restrictions on domestic production or consumption', as required by Article XX(g). The report of the panel was adopted in 1982. Interestingly, in 1981 Canada and the United States signed a Treaty on Pacific Coast Albacore Tuna Vessels and Port Privileges, effectively resolving the issue bilaterally between the two parties.

The next TREMs case was a 1987 panel on a complaint brought by Canada, the EC and Mexico against US taxes on petroleum and certain imported substances levied under the US 'Superfund' legislation (a federal programme to clean up hazardous waste). In line with the complainants' claims, the panel found that the imported and domestic petroleum products were 'like products' within the meaning of GATT Article III:2 and that the higher rate of tax imposed on the imported petroleum (3.5 cents per barrel higher) resulted in less favourable treatment to the imported product than the like domestic product in violation of Article III:2. In so finding, the panel noted that Article III:2 obliges contracting parties to establish certain competitive conditions for imported products *vis-à-vis* domestic products without reference to 'trade effects', and that the presumption that illegal measures caused nullification or impairment in terms of Article XXIII had operated in GATT practice as an irrefutable presumption. As to the taxes on other imported substances, the panel found that they did not discriminate against imported products and were eligible for border tax adjustment at the option of the importing party. In this connection, it noted that the GATT's rules on border tax adjustment thus gave the contracting party the possibility of following the Polluter Pays Principle, but did not oblige it to do so. The panel report was adopted in 1987.

A third panel report, adopted in 1988, involved a US complaint against Canadian export restrictions on unprocessed herring and salmon, introduced on the basis of Canada's Fisheries Act for reasons of fisheries conservation. The panel concluded that the export prohibitions were contrary to GATT Article XI:1 and were not justified under Article XX(b) or Article XX(g). Its reasoning was that, given the purpose of Article XX(g) of ensuring that the commitments under the GATT do not hinder the pursuit of policies aimed at the conservation of exhaustible natural resources, a trade measure had to be 'primarily aimed at' the conservation of such resources to be considered as 'relating to' conservation within the meaning of that provision; and that the measure had to be 'primarily aimed at' rendering effective restrictions on domestic production or consumption to be considered to be 'in conjunction with' such domestic restrictions, as required by the same provision. The panel found that the Canadian measure was neither primarily aimed at conservation nor primarily aimed at rendering effective domestic restrictions on production or consumption, and that therefore it could not be justified as a measure meeting the criteria of Article XX(g).

A fourth GATT panel dealt with a US complaint against Thailand, alleging that Thailand's import restrictions on cigarettes were inconsistent with GATT Article XI:1 and that its internal excise, business and municipal taxes on cigarettes were inconsistent with GATT Articles III:1 and III:2. During the panel proceeding, and at the request of Thailand, the panel heard testimony from the World Health Organization on the health effects of cigarette consumption. The panel concluded that the failure of Thailand to grant import licences for cigarettes over a ten-year period amounted to an import restriction inconsistent with Article XI:1 and that this inconsistency could not be justified by Article XX(b) as a measure 'necessary to protect human ... life or health', notwithstanding the fact that this provision clearly allowed contracting parties to give priority to human health over trade liberalization. It was found that the import restrictions imposed by Thailand could be considered to be 'necessary' in terms of Article XX(b) only if there were no alternative measure consistent with the GATT, or less inconsistent with it, which Thailand could reasonably be expected to employ to achieve its health policy objectives. In this particular case, Thailand's practice of permitting (and even encouraging) the sale of domestic cigarettes while not permitting the import of foreign cigarettes was an inconsistency with the GATT that was not 'necessary' within the meaning of Article XX(b). As regards Thailand's internal taxes on cigarettes, the regulations were found to be consistent with Thailand's national treatment obligations under Article III. The report of the panel was adopted by the GATT Council in 1990.

The fifth and sixth GATT disputes involving TREMs are better known as 'Tuna I' and 'Tuna II'. Tuna I was a 1991 complaint by Mexico against US import restrictions on tuna, imposed on the basis of the US Marine Mammal Protection Act (MMPA) restrictions on fish or products from fish caught with commercial fishing technology that resulted in the incidental killing or serious injury of ocean mammals in excess of US standards. The complaint, alleging inconsistency with Articles XI and XIII, was directed against a direct embargo on imports of tuna products from Mexico that were caught with purse seine nets in the high seas, an intermediary nation embargo on tuna products from any other country if the tuna was harvested with purse seine nets in the eastern tropical Pacific Ocean by Mexican vessels, and the voluntary use of the label 'Dolphin Safe', based on the US Dolphin Protection Consumer Act. The United States defended that the measure was a non-discriminatory border adjustment implementing an internal product regulation consistently with Article III and, alternatively, that it could be justified under Article XX(b), (d) or (g).

The panel ruled that the direct import prohibition on tuna products from Mexico was inconsistent with Article XI:1 and did not constitute an internal product regulation. As to the Article XX(b) defence, the Panel considered that this provision did not permit an 'extra-jurisdictional' protection of life and health to the effect that imports could be restricted whenever the life or health protection policies in the exporting country were not identical with those in the importing country. The US measures also were not 'necessary' in terms of Article XX(b) in that the US had not demonstrated to the panel that it had exhausted all options reasonably available to it to pursue its dolphin protection objectives through measures consistent with the GATT, in particular through the negotiation of international cooperative arrangements. Moreover, the US import restrictions were based on such unpredictable conditions (the incidental dolphin-taking rate actually recorded for US fishermen during the same period) that they could not be regarded as necessary to the protection of dolphins. The panel then found that the same considerations that led it to reject an extra-jurisdictional application of Article XX(b) applied also to Article XX(g). The panel went on to reject the intermediary nation embargo on the same grounds, as well as finding that this latter measure also could not be justified under Article XX(d) as a measure necessary to secure compliance with laws or regulations not inconsistent with the GATT. In its concluding remarks, the panel noted that the GATT imposed few constraints on members' implementation of domestic environmental policies or on their right to cooperate with one another in harmonizing such policies, or for that matter on the right of the contracting parties acting jointly to address international environmental problems by amending, supplementing or waiving GATT obligations. Owing to opposition by the United States, no consensus was reached on adopting the panel report.

Tuna II was another complaint against US import restrictions on tuna, this time initiated by the EC and the Netherlands on behalf of the Netherlands Antilles. The measures at issue here were again a primary nation embargo, affecting direct imports of tuna harvested by a method resulting in the incidental killing or serious injury of marine mammals in excess of US standards, and an intermediary nation embargo against nations that exported yellowfin tuna to the United States or imported tuna that were subject to the direct nation embargo, imposed pursuant to the MMPA.

In issuing its report in 1994, the panel found that both types of embargo were inconsistent with Article XI:1 since they banned the import of tuna from any country not meeting certain policy conditions. Article III was not applicable because the US measures could not affect the product as such, and because they accorded less favourable treatment to like products not produced in conformity with domestic policies of the importing country. The panel went on to find that the import restrictions could not be justified under Article XX(b) or (g) since measures that were taken so as to force other countries to change their policies, and were effective only if such changes occurred, were neither 'necessary' for the protection of animal life or health (Article XX(b)) nor 'primarily aimed at' the conservation of an exhaustible natural resource or rendering effective restrictions on domestic production or consumption (Article XX(g)). Again, in its concluding observations, the panel observed that the issue in dispute was not the validity of the environmental objectives of the United States to protect and conserve dolphins. The issue was whether, in the pursuit of its environmental objectives, the United States could impose trade embargoes to secure changes in the policies that other contracting parties pursued within their own jurisdiction. The panel could find nothing to support the view that contracting parties, by agreeing to give one another in Article XX the right to take trade measures necessary to protect the health and life of plants, animals and persons, or aimed at the conservation of exhaustible natural resources, had agreed to accord one another the right to impose trade embargoes for such purposes. Adoption of the report was blocked by the United States.

The seventh (and last) GATT panel involving a TREM was based on a complaint by the European Community, in March 1993, against three different US measures on automobiles: a luxury tax, a gas guzzler tax, and Corporate Average Fuel Economy (CAFE) regulations. The panel first noted that Article III serves only to prohibit regulatory distinctions between products applied so as to afford protection to domestic production; its purpose is not to prohibit fiscal and regulatory distinctions applied so as to achieve other policy goals. It went on to rule that the luxury tax, which applied to cars sold for over $30,000, was not a measure discriminating between 'like' imported and domestic products since neither the principal aim nor the effect of the threshold distinction of $30,000 was to create conditions of competition that divided products inherently into two classes, one of EC or other foreign origin and the other of domestic origin. Accordingly, there was no inconsistency with the national treatment provisions of Article III:2. On similar reasoning, the panel found that the gas guzzler tax, which applied to the sale of automobiles with low fuel economy (below 22.5 miles per gallon), was not a distinction between 'like products' because neither the aim nor the effect of the fiscal measure was to change conditions of competition affording protection to US production. Again, therefore, Article III:2 was not implicated.

Finally, with respect to the CAFE regulations, which required the average fuel economy for passenger cars manufactured in the United States or sold by any importer not to fall below 27.5 miles per gallon, the panel found these regulations to be inconsistent with Article III:4 because the foreign fleet accounting discriminated against foreign cars and the fleet averaging methodology differentiated between imported and domestic like products on the basis of factors relating to control or ownership of producer or importers, rather than on the basis of factors directly related to the products as such, thus affording less favourable conditions of competition to products of foreign origin. The panel then rejected the US defence as to fleet accounting under Article XX(g), finding that the separate foreign fleet accounting was not primarily aimed at the conservation of natural resources; the panel did not make a finding on the US Article XX(g) defence concerning the fleet averaging methodology. The report of the panel, circulated in 1994, was not adopted because of opposition from the European Community.

Following the entry into force of the WTO Agreement on 1 January 1995, the first case considered under the new WTO dispute settlement system involved a TREM. This was a complaint brought by Venezuela and Brazil against US standards for reformulated and conventional gasoline. At issue were minimum standards for gasoline quality, promulgated under the US Clean Air Act, to reduce air pollution from automobile emissions (the 'Gasoline Rule'). The WTO panel found that the baseline establishment methods treated imported gasoline less favourably than like domestic gasoline, in violation of GATT Article III:4. The panel further found that this discrimination in baseline methodology could not be justified under Article XX(b) because it was not 'necessary' to the achievement of the policy objective of improving air quality, or under Article XX(d) because it did not 'secure compliance' with the baseline system, or under Article XX(g) because there was no direct connection between the less favourable treatment of imported gasoline and the US objective of improving air quality.

This case then became the first dispute appealed to the WTO Appellate Body. The United States only requested review of the panel's ruling under Article XX(g). On this issue, the Appellate Body defined the 'measures' subject to justification under Article XX(g) more broadly than had the panel, finding that the justification should be examined as to the entire baseline establishment rules of the US Gasoline Rule, not only their discriminatory provisions which were found to be inconsistent with Article III:4. This broader interpretation then led the Appellate Body to conclude that the measures were primarily aimed at conservation and at rendering effective domestic restrictions. But the Appellate Body went on to analyse the introductory 'chapeau' or headnote to Article XX, finding that the baseline establishment rules constituted unjustifiable discrimination and a disguised restriction on international trade, and therefore were not justified under Article XX(g). The Appellate Body report and the panel report (as modified) were adopted by the DSB in May 1996.

These eight cases are the only ones to date involving trade-related environmental measures for which panels have completed their work and issued reports. However, in addition three other TREM panels have been established in the WTO, and two further such panels are likely to be established very soon.

Two of these additional cases involve separate complaints by the United States and Canada against the European Community over measures affecting meat and meat products (hormones). Complainants claim that the EC measures, taken under the Council Directive Prohibiting the Use in Livestock Farming of Certain Substances having a Hormonal Action, restrict or prohibit imports of meat and meat products in violation of GATT Articles III or XI, SPS Agreement Articles 2, 3 and 5, and TBT Agreement Article 2. In these cases, the panels have sought advice from a number of scientific experts, including one from the Codex Alimentarius Commission. The panels are expected to issue their reports shortly.

The third case is a panel established in February 1997 at the request of Malaysia, Pakistan and Thailand to consider their complaint against a US import prohibition of shrimp and shrimp products. India has since requested establishment of a panel on the same issue. The matter concerns a US ban on imports of shrimp from these countries owing to their failure to comply with provisions of the US Endangered Species Act requiring protection of sea turtles. The complaining parties invoke GATT Articles I, XI and XIII. It is interesting to note that, unlike the tuna cases mentioned above, this shrimp/turtle case at least indirectly implicates an MEA, specifically the Convention on International Trade in Endangered Species (CITES) under which various species of sea turtles are listed.

On the immediate horizon are two more TREMs cases concerning complaints by Canada and the United States against Australian measures affecting the import of salmon. Complainants allege that the prohibition on imports of salmon based on a quarantine regulation is inconsistent with GATT Articles XI and XIII and the SPS Agreement. It is likely that at least one panel on this matter (the Canadian complaint) will be established in April 1997.

Conclusions

The multilateral trading rules of the WTO and national/multilateral trade-related environmental policies will inevitably continue to evolve alongside one another. The challenge and responsibility of member governments, international organizations and concerned citizens is to ensure that this evolution proceeds on a mutually compatible and sustainable basis and, if possible, on a mutually reinforcing basis. This will require intelligence, creativity, forethought and a truly cooperative spirit. Not an easy task. But much – to some extent even the sustainable development of the planet – may depend on its satisfactory fulfilment.

Discussion

Participants in the discussion agreed on the importance of the continued evolution of the WTO's dispute settlement system. It was felt that successive GATT and WTO panels had gradually become more sensitized to environmental concerns – particularly evident in the Reformulated Gasoline case, with the Appellate Body's broader interpretation of GATT Article XX(g), and in the pending Beef Hormones dispute, where the panel had sought scientific advice. Mr Gertler felt this was part of a general rise in environmental awareness among WTO members as much as panels, and probably was due to an improved exchange of information between the various government departments involved.

Editor's note:
Of the additional dispute cases referred to in this section, the two beef hormone panels reported on 18 August 1997; after an appeal by the EU, the Appellate Body reported on 16 January 1998. The shrimp-turtle panel reported on 6 April 1998; at the time of writing, it seems likely that this case will also be referred to the Appellate Body. A panel was established in the Canada–Australia salmon dispute on 10 April 1997, and has yet to report.

Chapter 5

Conclusion: The Future

The final session of the conference featured a panel discussion with six participants considering the likely future direction for the trade and environment debate, and the role of the WTO, and particularly the CTE, within it. Each of the speakers gave brief statements, which are reproduced below; some of the papers included here are in fact longer versions of the necessarily short presentations. The chapter concludes with a summary of the ensuing discussion.

5.1 Trade and environment in the WTO[84]
Sabrina Shaw

Background to WTO work on trade and environment

When trade ministers approved the results of the Uruguay Round negotiations in Marrakesh in April 1994, they also took a decision to begin a comprehensive work programme on trade and environment in the WTO. Their decision ensured that the subject has been given, and will continue to be given, a high profile on the WTO agenda.

The issue of trade and environment was not included for negotiation in the Uruguay Round, but certain environmental concerns were nevertheless addressed in the results of the negotiations. The preamble to the WTO Agreement includes direct references to the objective of sustainable development and to the need to protect and preserve the environment. The new Agreements on Technical Barriers to Trade and on the Application of Sanitary and Phytosanitary Measures explicitly take into account the use

---

[84] The views expressed in this paper are my own and should not be attributed to WTO members.

by governments of measures to protect human, animal and plant life and health and the environment. The Agreement on Agriculture exempts direct payments under environmental programmes from WTO members' commitments to reduce domestic support for agricultural production, subject to certain conditions. The Agreement on Subsidies and Countervailing Measures treats as a non-actionable subsidy government assistance to industry covering up to 20% of the cost of adapting existing facilities to new environmental legislation. And both the TRIPS and the Services Agreements contain environment-related provisions. More generally, and as was recognized in the results of the UN Conference on Environment and Development in 1992 (the 'Earth Summit'), an open, equitable and non-discriminatory multilateral trading system has a key contribution to make to national and international efforts to better protect and conserve environmental resources and to promote sustainable development.

The WTO Committee on Trade and Environment has brought environmental and sustainable development issues into the mainstream of WTO work. The Committee's first report, which was submitted to the WTO Ministerial Conference in Singapore, notes that the WTO is interested in building a constructive relationship between trade and environmental concerns. Trade and environment are both important areas of policy-making and they should be mutually supportive in order to promote sustainable development. The multilateral trading system has the capacity to further integrate environmental considerations and enhance its contribution to the promotion of sustainable development without undermining its open, equitable and non-discriminatory character.

The Marrakesh Ministerial Decision on Trade and Environment

Trade ministers in Marrakesh agreed to establish a WTO Committee on Trade and Environment with a broadly based remit covering all areas of the multilateral trading system – goods, services and intellectual property. The CTE has been given both analytical and prescriptive functions: to identify the relationships between trade and environmental measures in order to promote sustainable development, and to make recommendations on whether any modifications to the provisions of the multilateral trading system are required. The CTE forwarded its first report on its work to the WTO Ministerial Conference in Singapore.

Two important parameters have guided the CTE's work. One is that WTO competence for policy coordination in this area is limited to trade and those trade-related aspects of environmental policies that may result in significant trade effects for its members. In other words, there is no intention that the WTO should become an environmental agency, or that it should get involved in reviewing national environmental priorities, setting environmental standards or developing global policies on the environment: that will continue to be the task of national governments and of other inter-governmental organizations better suited to the task. The second parameter is that, if problems of policy coordination to protect the environment and promote sustainable development are identified through the CTE's work, steps taken to resolve them must uphold and safeguard the principles of the multilateral trading system which governments spent seven years strengthening and improving through the Uruguay Round negotiations.

The CTE's work programme was set out initially in ten areas. A start on the work programme was made soon after the Marrakesh ministerial meeting, under the authority of the WTO Preparatory Committee, and from 1 January 1995, with the coming into force of the WTO Agreement, the Committee on Trade and Environment was formally established to continue work in this area. The CTE process has been driven by proposals from individual WTO members on issues of importance to them. The CTE adopted its report on 8 November 1996 and it has been forwarded through the General Council to Ministers at the Ministerial Conference.[85]

The following is a brief review of the items of the CTE's work programme. A more detailed discussion and the conclusions and recommendations to ministers are contained in the CTE's Report to the Ministerial Conference.

---

[85] The Report (WT/CTE/1, dated 12 November 1996) is available from the WTO Secretariat and can be accessed at the following Internet address: http://www.wto.org/Trade+Env/tocte.html.

The relationship between the provisions of the multilateral trading system and trade measures for environmental purposes, including those pursuant to multilateral environmental agreements

A range of provisions in the WTO can accommodate the use of trade-related measures needed for environmental purposes, including measures taken pursuant to MEAs. Those that are cited regularly as being of key importance are the provisions relating to non-discrimination (MFN and national treatment) and transparency. Beyond that, and subject to certain important conditions, the exceptions clauses contained in Article XX of the GATT allow a WTO member legitimately to place its public health and safety and national environmental goals ahead of its general obligation not to raise trade restrictions or to apply discriminatory trade measures. These provisions have been a major focus of work of the CTE and will be kept under review in the future work programme.

Trade measures applied pursuant to MEAs

One area of particular focus in the CTE's discussion has been the relationship between WTO provisions and trade measures applied pursuant to MEAs. It has been clear throughout the discussions on this issue in the GATT/WTO that the preferred approach for governments to take in tackling transboundary or global environmental problems is cooperative, multilateral action under an MEA. That was the approach endorsed by political leaders at the highest level in 1992 at the UNCED, and its appeal is quite evident from the point of view of the WTO which is dedicated to finding cooperative, multilateral solutions to problems in the area of trade. In the CTE Report, WTO members state that the WTO supports multilateral solutions to global and transboundary environmental problems and that unilateral actions in this context should be avoided.

While some MEAs contain trade provisions, the report notes that trade restrictions are not the only, or even necessarily the most effective, policy instrument to use in MEAs, but that in certain cases they can play an important role. It also states that the WTO already provides broad and valuable scope for trade measures to be applied pursuant to MEAs in a WTO-consistent manner. To date, few MEAs contain trade provisions and no problem has arisen in the WTO over the use of trade measures applied pursuant to MEAs. A number of proposals have been put forward in the CTE to broaden the scope available under WTO provisions for the use of trade measures applied pursuant to MEAs, including some that would create an 'environmental window' for the use of discriminatory trade measures against non-parties to MEAs; but these proposals have not attracted consensus support in the CTE.

Dispute settlement

A related item concerns the appropriate forum for the settlement of potential disputes that may arise over the use of trade measures pursuant to MEAs; is it the WTO, or the dispute settlement mechanisms that exist in the MEAs themselves? There is general agreement that, in the event of a dispute arising between WTO members who are each parties to an MEA over the use of trade measures that they are applying among themselves pursuant to the MEA, they should consider in the first instance trying to resolve it through the dispute settlement mechanisms available under the MEA. Were a dispute to arise with a non-party to an MEA, however, the WTO would provide the only possible forum for the settlement of the dispute.

In the Report, WTO members note that better policy coordination between trade and environmental policy officials at the national level can help prevent situations from arising in which the use of trade measures applied pursuant to MEAs could become subject to disputes. Furthermore, they note that problems are unlikely to arise in the WTO over trade measures agreed and applied among parties to a MEA. In the event of a dispute, however, WTO members are confident that the WTO dispute settlement provisions would be able to tackle any problems that arise in this area, including cases where resort to environmental expertise is needed.

Ecolabelling

Ecolabelling programmes are important environmental policy instruments. Ecolabelling was discussed extensively in the GATT, and those discussions laid the basis in the CTE for a detailed examination of the issues involved. The key requirement from the WTO's point of view is that environmental measures that incorporate trade provisions or that affect trade significantly do not discriminate between home-produced goods and imports, or between imports from and exports to different trading partners. Non-discrimination is the cornerstone of secure and predictable market access and undistorted competition: it guarantees consumer choice, and it gives producers access to the full range of market opportunities. Subject to that requirement being met, WTO rules place essentially no constraints on the policy choices available to a country to protect its own environment against damage either from domestic production or from the consumption of domestically produced or imported products.

The CTE Report states that well-designed ecolabelling programmes can be effective instruments of environmental policy. It notes that in certain cases they have raised significant concerns about their possible trade effects. An important starting point for addressing some of those trade concerns is to ensure adequate transparency in their preparation, adoption and application, including affording opportunities for participation in their preparation by interested parties from other countries. Further discussion is needed on how the use in ecolabelling programmes of criteria based on non-product-related processes and production methods should be treated under the rules of the WTO Agreement on Technical Barriers to Trade.

WTO transparency provisions

WTO transparency provisions fulfil an important role in ensuring the proper functioning of the multilateral trading system, in helping to prevent unnecessary trade restriction and distortion from occurring, in providing information about market opportunities and in helping to avoid trade disputes from arising. They can also provide a valuable first step in ensuring that trade and environment policies are developed and implemented in a mutually supportive way. Trade-related environmental measures should not be required to meet more onerous transparency requirements than other measures that affect trade. The CTE Report states that no modifications to WTO rules are required to ensure adequate transparency for trade-related environmental measures. The WTO Secretariat will compile from the Central Registry of Notifications all notifications of trade-related environmental measures and will collate these in a single database which can be accessed by WTO members.

The issue of the export of domestically prohibited goods

Concerns were raised by a number of developing-country GATT contracting parties in the mid-1980s that certain hazardous or toxic products were being exported to them without their being fully informed about the environmental or public health dangers that the products could pose. In the late 1980s a GATT Working Party examined ways of treating trade in goods that are severely restricted or banned for sale on the domestic market of the exporting country. A key consideration was that the importing country should be fully informed about the products it was receiving and should have the right to reject them if it felt they would cause it environmental or public health problems.

In the period since the GATT Working Party ended its discussions, several MEAs have been negotiated to deal with problems of trade in environmentally hazardous products (e.g. the Basel Convention and London Guidelines). The WTO does not intend to duplicate work that has already been accomplished elsewhere in the area of domestically prohibited goods.

In the CTE Report, WTO members agree to support the efforts of the specialized intergovernmental environmental organizations that are helping to resolve the problems that exist. However, they note that there may be a complementary role for the WTO to play in this area. As an initial step, the Secretariat will survey the information already available in the WTO on trade in domestically prohibited goods.

Trade liberalization and sustainable development

Further liberalization of international trade flows, in both goods and services, has a key role to play in advancing economic policy objectives in member countries. In that respect, WTO member countries have already made an important contribution to sustainable development and better environmental protection world-wide through the conclusion of the Uruguay Round negotiations. This contribution will steadily increase as the results of the Round move towards full implementation. The UNCED also recognized an open, non-discriminatory trading system to be a prerequisite for effective action to protect the environment and to generate sustainable development. This is based on the perspective that countries, particularly developing countries, are dependent on trade as the main source of continued growth and prosperity.

The CTE is tackling this item of its work programme in the context of the built-in agenda for further trade liberalization initiatives contained in the results of the Uruguay Round negotiations. In its Report, the CTE notes that the removal of trade restrictions and distortions, in particular high tariffs, tariff escalation, export restrictions, subsidies and non-tariff barriers, has the potential to yield benefits for both the multilateral trading system and the environment. Further analytical and empirical work will take place on this issue.

Trade in services and TRIPS

The Marrakesh Decision calls for the CTE to examine the role of the WTO in relation to the links between environmental measures and the new trade agreements reached in the Uruguay Round negotiations on services and intellectual property. Discussions on these two items of the work programme have broken new ground since there was very little understanding of how the rules of the trading system might affect or be affected by environmental policies in these areas.

With respect to the General Agreement on Trade in Services (GATS) and the environment, the Report notes that discussions in the CTE have not led to the identification of any measures that members feel may be applied for environmental purposes to services trade which are not already adequately covered by GATS provisions, in particular in Article XIV (b).

In the case of intellectual property, WTO members state in the CTE Report that the Agreement on Trade-Related Aspects of Intellectual Property Rights (TRIPS) plays an essential role in facilitating access to and transfer of environmentally sound technology and products. However, they have noted that further work will be required in this area, including on clarifying the relationship between the TRIPS Agreement and the Convention on Biological Diversity.

Further work

WTO members believe that work in the WTO on contributing to build a constructive relationship between trade, environment and sustainable development needs to continue. They have recommended, therefore, that the CTE should continue its work, reporting to the WTO General Council, with the same mandate and terms of reference that were given it by Ministers in Marrakesh in 1994.

5.2 Industry perspective
   Reinhard Quick

I wish to concentrate on three flashpoints, put into the context of the trade and environment debate:

1.   Sustainable development;
2.   The importance of the rule of law;
3.   The notion of sovereignty.

The notion of sustainable development and an agreed-upon interpretation

If we could find common ground on what this means, and how it could be interpreted, we might have fewer trade and environment arguments. There must be sufficient guarantees that economic, ecological and society's needs will be given equal treatment, since neglect of any one component, or undue concentration on one of the components, will jeopardize sustainable development as such. Therefore, there is no primacy of trade over the environment, and there is no primacy of environment over trade.

As an example with respect to MEAs, the Basel Convention and the Montreal Protocol are in conflict with the WTO. If one applies the notion of sustainable development to these cases, one might conclude that the trade measures of the Montreal Protocol are sustainable whereas some trade measures of the Basel Convention, in particular those with respect to the export prohibition on dangerous waste for recycling, are unsustainable. The solution of the potential conflict between MEAs and the WTO could therefore lie in the accommodation of those trade measures that are 'sustainable' even if they are discriminatory in the traditional GATT sense. Notwithstanding the reluctance of the WTO membership to continue to look for a compromise with respect to MEAs, the issue is of importance because a result would give negotiators of MEAs some useful guidelines on when trade measures are feasible or not.

The importance of the rule of law

The international legal system has seen an enormous development in the last fifty years The system is devised to solve conflicts by adjudication and conciliation and not by the rule of force. Attention will therefore be given to the question of compliance with international rulings.

WTO members are obliged to implement the rulings of the WTO dispute settlement process. They do not immediately have the alternative to ignore the ruling and pay compensation or face retaliation. It is therefore necessary to stress the notion of the rule of law and to remind our legislators that they have ratified the WTO with all its rights and obligations.

Another feature in this context is dispute settlement avoidance. WTO members need to put more emphasis on compliance with WTO laws when drafting legislation. It is quite astonishing that the draft End-of-Life Vehicles Directive contains a ban on certain products that are otherwise not banned in the European Union. How can one justify an explicit discrimination between PVC in cars and PVC in Barbie dolls?

The Biodiversity Convention and the TRIPS Agreement both contain rights and obligations for their members and there is a potential conflict between the two. Because some do not like the legal requirements of TRIPS, should one therefore go so far as they do and say: 'All countries, particularly developing-country governments, may wish to delay any patent law over life forms until the current ambiguities or uncertainties are resolved'? We will incite conflict if we invite members of a certain legal regime to behave illegally. TRIPS is a chance and not a danger for developing countries; the agreement leaves them sufficient room to take into account their national situation and their quest for development.

Sovereignty

The fundamental question is: how has the notion of sovereignty developed over the last fifty years, and can we deduce from this development that the GATT product/process distinction is still, or is no longer, valid in today's world?

While we have to recognize some development in the notion of sovereignty, we cannot yet deduce that a sovereign nation can impose on another sovereign nation how it should produce a certain product, and enforce its rule with an import prohibition while allowing domestic production of the same product. Therefore the basic GATT distinction remains valid, and with good reason – namely, to protect the WTO membership against protectionist abuse.

Nevertheless, I expect some further developments. WTO panels will in the long run interpret the concept of 'like product' more flexibly to accommodate environmental concerns. There will also be increased negotiation of MEAs with specific obligations concerning the production process or environmental management as such.

5.3 Developing-country perspective[86]
Magda Shahin

This theme is not an easy one. Following mainly the debate on trade and environment taking place in the WTO, there are a number of questions I will try to raise at the outset without promising any answers for many of them. Some can be answered in a straightforward manner, others will necessitate additional thinking and further analysis on our part. Let me start by raising the following questions:

---

[86] These comments are based on Magda Shahin, *Trade and Environment in the WTO: Achievements and Future Prospects* (Penang: Third World Network, 1997).

- Is the WTO an adequate forum for a continued debate on the interface between trade and environment for trade as well as environmental experts, or has its glamour and relevancy faded away, at least for the environmentalists?
- Do the environmentalists still want to use the so-called policeman of the multilateral trading system to advance the environmental debate?
- Will developing countries forgo the integration of developmental aspects in the WTO?
- Will the debate in the WTO be superseded by fora such as the Commission on Sustainable Development, MEAs or even UNCTAD, where a freer debate is possible, delinked from commitments of rights and obligations, and from possible additional criteria to ensure the consistency of trade measures for environmental purposes?
- Have such measures in the first place proved necessary and effective for the protection of the environment?
- Are the so-called legalistic issues, such as the relationship between MEAs and the WTO, or the PPMs issue in the framework of ecolabelling and its coverage by the TBT Agreement, still alive and dynamic?
- Is there still some room for manoeuvre with a view to possibly reaching some concrete results in this respect, or will the future debate in the CTE be a repetitive one?

In a preliminary attempt to answer some of these questions and leave many for our collective thinking and for later discussion, let me stress that, in my view, the WTO will continue to be seized with the issue of the relationship between trade and environment at least for the foreseeable future.

The Singapore Ministerial in December 1996 has ensured the place of the Committee on Trade and Environment in the WTO. Paragraph 219, entitled 'Future of the CTE', is the last paragraph of the report submitted to the Ministers. It clearly asserts that work in the WTO on the relationship between trade, environment and sustainable development needs to continue and directs the CTE to continue its work – reporting to the General Council – under its existing mandate and terms of reference, as contained in the Ministerial Decision on Trade and Environment of April 1994. Hence the CTE has become an integral and regular part of the work in the WTO, after being kept on the periphery with an uncertain future for two years after Marrakesh.

Becoming an integral part of WTO certainly has its pros and cons for the future of the entire debate on trade and environment. One can say, on the one hand, that the debate may lose some of its political attractiveness and appeal of the last two years, as now the CTE will follow the regular course of work like any other committee in the WTO that usually meets twice or three times a year at the maximum. On the other hand, it will certainly gain by becoming an integral part of the WTO framework of rights and obligations, in the sense that, sooner or later, the contracting parties will see themselves obliged to go into 'negotiating' clear guidelines, disciplines and criteria – if need be – for how and where to place the environment with its multiplicity of issues in the framework of WTO rules and regulations – a highly controversial issue which was debated at length throughout the last two years. This may even occur sooner than we expect. I believe that, in view of the forthcoming 'substantive' Ministerial which is expected by the end of 1999, trade and environment will become part of the so-called new 'mini round', which will include, among others, negotiations in the areas of agriculture, services, investment and competition policies.

Informally, the members of the Committee have agreed to group the ten items of the agenda into two main clusters. The first cluster, which is going to be taken up in the May 1997 meeting of the CTE, will focus on the effect of environmental measures on market access, as well as ecolabelling and the relationship between the TRIPS Agreement and the environment, including the transfer of environmentally sound technology. The second cluster, which is to be taken up at the second meeting, is devoted to the relationship between MEAs and the WTO. A third meeting by the end of 1997 will take up the leftovers or so-called unfinished business. An important innovation, which should not pass unnoticed, is the annual NGO symposium aimed at promoting a constructive and sensible dialogue between delegations and NGO representatives on issues related to trade, environment and sustainable development; approximately 50 NGOs from developing and developed countries representing business, environmental and developmental organizations will be invited to participate and speak on a whole range of issues and areas of the CTE's programme of work.

Building on the conclusions and recommendations of the report submitted to Ministers, one should attempt to anticipate where at least the focus of the current discussion might possibly lie, in order to move the entire debate forward. This will also certainly have to be based on the premiss that environmentalists as well as 'tradeists' from both developed and developing countries are ready and willing to work together in good faith, and, what is even more important, to be aware of one another's sensitivities.

The relationship between MEAs and the WTO

In my view the debate on the relationship between MEAs and the WTO in its various aspects has been dealt with extensively throughout the two-year work of the Committee. Clear guidance was given in the CTE report, especially with regard to the following:

1. There is considerable scope for members to use trade measures for environmental purposes consistent with WTO rules, including the defined scope of Article XX. It has also been emphasized in this context that this accommodation is valuable and it is important that it be preserved by all. *In other words, there is no consensus on a need to go beyond existing WTO provisions to accommodate trade provisions taken in the context of or pursuant to MEAs.*
2. It is very unlikely that parties to a MEA would challenge trade measures taken pursuant to MEAs, as that would undermine the obligations they have accepted, as clearly stated in para. 178 of the report. The same paragraph goes on giving some kind of implicit encouragement to parties to consider trying to resolve disputes over the use of trade measures they are applying between themselves pursuant to the MEA through the dispute settlement mechanisms available under the MEA.

Though these two conclusions would seem to many to be as evident and obvious as possible, they were not easy to reach. Nevertheless, I would agree with those who would question the time and effort consumed on this. I would go even further and ask whether we were having a false debate all the time. *MEAs have coexisted and will continue to coexist with the WTO.* Up to now, there has been no GATT or WTO dispute concerning trade measures applied pursuant to a MEA. That does not mean, however, that all trade measures taken pursuant to MEAs are consistent with GATT provisions. For instance, trade measures in the Basel Convention or in CITES can certainly become an issue in WTO, but what needs to be stressed is that it is very unlikely for a MEA party, having conceded certain obligations in one forum, to raise the problem in another forum, i.e. the WTO. On this the CTE report has urged better coordination at the national level to ensure that no conflicting obligations are being undertaken by governments in two separate multilateral fora and to ensure that WTO members respect the commitments they have made in the separate fora of the WTO and MEAs.

It is not difficult, however, to assess that one of the remaining sticking points in this complex relationship is the use of discriminatory measures against non-parties to an MEA. This will make it incumbent upon us to address the issue of 'the definition of MEAs' in a more decisive manner, which in my view is most relevant and lies at the heart of the debate. So far the issue remains unresolved and developed countries continue to question the need for such a definition. If we have universal or quasi-universal MEAs, the non-party issue becomes less of a problem. The issue becomes more controversial for new MEAs if the membership is limited. Hence the non-party issue could be expected to generate tension in the future.

Another major point for developing and developed countries alike that will continue to attract a heated debate is how to deal with unilateralism and extraterritorial measures. Though the report has again endorsed Principle 12 of the Rio Declaration, this was as far as the CTE could go on this very controversial and highly sensitive issue for the United States. The 'shrimp/turtle case' submitted as a dispute by Thailand, Malaysia, Pakistan and India against the United States in the WTO recently will be another case in point after the tuna/dolphin case where the panel and the Appellate Body will have to set the tone for how the WTO should go about extraterritorial measures. It is surely more valuable to have measures based on internationally agreed principles than on unilateral measures.

In my view, more important than the results of the panel or the Appellate Body will be the debate this case will revive in the WTO on *the necessity of the trade measures*: the proportionality aspect, and the nature of 'least trade-restrictive'. The effectiveness of the trade measures could also be raised in such a debate, a criterion which so far has been avoided by panels. The discussion of such criteria has faced strong resistance in last year's discussion. They were, however, brought up by New Zealand in its position paper submitted to the CTE, and should certainly be the focus of our future debate, if only for the sake of their clarification. Also, the environmental community has to come to grips with these concepts, if it still wants to integrate the environment as a legitimate trade-related problem in the WTO. Such substantive criteria, if agreed upon, would help ensure that measures necessary for environmental purposes were not unnecessarily disruptive of the multilateral trading system in achieving the environmental objective. They could further ensure that legitimate environmental protection measures can be taken while safeguarding against protectionist abuse and preserving an open, equitable and non-discriminatory multilateral trading system.

The last issue that remains open in this complex relationship is the assessment of the implementation of positive measures in the framework of MEAs, such as market access, capacity building, access to and transfer of technology. The important role of positive measures in MEAs is also recognized in paras. 173 and 207 of the CTE report. This is another issue that should be pushed in this domain. The point is, though, how far can the debate on positive measures be pushed in the WTO, and, if not far, how can we ensure a comprehensive and balanced approach in MEAs? To that end UNCTAD has already decided to convene an expert group in November 1997.

The relationship between the multilateral trading system and ecolabelling

On ecolabelling the following three issues were debated at length:

1. the coverage and applicability of the TBT Agreement;
2. the transparency aspect;
3. the trade effects of ecolabelling.

The transparency aspects have been extensively addressed and were the least of the problem. The CTE has agreed that the transparency provisions contained in the TBT Agreement, including the Code of Good Practice, provide *a reference point* to the further work of the Committee in enhancing transparency for ecolabelling schemes or programmes. It also concluded further down, under the item of transparency, that no modifications to WTO rules were required to ensure adequate transparency for existing trade-related environmental measures (i.e. no blank cheque was given for future trade-related environmental measures). Two questions remain, however: how much is ecolabelling a trade-related measure, and, if it is, does ecolabelling count under existing or future trade-related environmental measures? Though transparency provisions by themselves were considered adequate, such questions certainly remain to be settled. Also, compliance by members with the notification procedures continues to be debatable. Canada presses for notification, irrespective of the issue of coverage and application of the TBT Agreement to ecolabelling. Whether this will be confirmed is still not known, as some would continue to argue that accepting the TBT provisions for ecolabelling – even if only for transparency purposes – might have implications for the PPMs issue. In addition, one might expect that the EU may continue to push for a Code of Good Practice devoted solely to ecolabelling.

What will continue to be subject of high tension, however, will be the debate on the legality of the issue of process and production methods (PPMs). I am deeply convinced that it will be very difficult to forge any kind of consensus in this respect, as developing countries not only will resist legitimizing environmental domestic policies and preferences in the WTO but also fear that this will have even more far-reaching implications in the future, as it could rebound on labour standards.

Furthermore, there is a widely acknowledged view that ecolabelling will die a natural death, if left to itself; its market potential is as yet not proven. Such a view only sustains and strengthens the position of developing countries in their legitimate concerns and doubts about the essence of triggering such a tedious debate in the CTE, at a time when other issues of more relevance to the interface between trade and environment are being put aside. It also raises the question of whether it is really ecolabelling, as an issue, that is at the heart of our debate, or rather, as indicated, it is PPMs that are becoming the sole target, putting into question the basic criteria and characteristics that have so far governed the multilateral trading system, and making ecolabelling the litmus test through which the WTO will become more and more deeply involved in the realm of domestic policy.

Questions were also raised about the relationship between the WTO and the ISO and why the WTO should endorse ISO guidelines – as has been proposed by Canada in the Committee. It is true that this is the way product standards have gone so far. The recognition in the TBT Agreement of ISO as a standard-setting body (Article 2.5) stems from the fact that it has dealt up to the present time with product-related PPMs based on performance and safety criteria. Hence, it would be inappropriate to equate such standards with non-related PPM criteria based on values and public policies that differ from one society to another, making it all the more difficult to internationalize PPMs.

A second route through which to consider ecolabelling schemes and programmes would be equivalencies and mutual recognition of national schemes and programmes. This is the route that is considered more appropriate from the economic side. Developing countries should stir the debate on equivalencies and mutual recognition, if ecolabelling continues to be an issue. These two routes (recognizing multilateral guidelines set outside the framework of WTO, and equivalencies and mutual recognition) are different. Whether we opt for either or for both remains a matter for further negotiations. At any rate, and for the future debate on this issue, it will be all the more important for developing countries to concentrate on clarifying questions such as the market potential of ecolabelling and its possible trade effects, and the role envisaged for the

WTO in ecolabelling, bearing in mind the underlying controversies in the sphere of competence of the WTO regarding the PPMs issue and whether it is justifiable to alter the very basis of the system for ecolabelling, an issue whose connection with, and relevance to, the trade system remains open.

The effect of environmental measures on market access

The debate on this issue from the perspective of developing countries tends to be twofold. One aspect is to ensure that existing market access conditions are not eroded by emerging environmental requirements. The other is to determine how additional market access – through what can be perceived as win–win situations – can help promote environmental protection and sustainable development. In addition, there is the tendency by some to bring back the debate on internalization of environmental externalities with all its complexities. I myself doubt that the WTO can turn its attention to this topic before further research and analysis is carried out.

To provide a focus to the future debate concerning the effects of environmental measures on market access, a topical issue for developing countries, and to consider what could be of more relevance in the WTO debate, I suggest a concentration on *a sectoral approach*, where effects and concerns varying between sectors and subject to various factors will have to be thoroughly addressed. It has been strongly argued on the part of the developing countries that the impact of environmental requirements on market access, though difficult to generalize, are visible and vary subject to a number of factors, including type of sector, together with socio-economic conditions, size of firms, economies of scale, infrastructure and access to technology. Focus should certainly be on identifying sectors of export interest to developing countries, such as textiles and clothing, leather, footwear, furniture and other consumer goods, where environmental measures could affect existing market access opportunities and thus possibly nullify the results of the Uruguay Round. Issues such as subsidies, tariff escalation and other trade-distortive measures are expected to figure high in the WTO debate. The Secretariat has already been mandated to prepare a background paper in this respect.

In this context, it would be essential for developing countries to stir the debate on sectors such as textiles and clothing, where we have lately witnessed so many trade measures for non-trade purposes being applied regularly by developed importing countries. We should also raise the very sensitive question of the environmental benefits accruing from removing trade restrictions and distortions and of whether this will urge reconsideration of the pace and the way in which the Agreement on Textiles and Clothing has so far been implemented. In other words, will this drive the developed importing countries to implement the Agreement in spirit and not only in letter (a repeated criticism by the exporting countries in the light of the fact that no commercially meaningful integration has been made to allow for improved market access, as agreed)? Might that be an issue for consideration? Might we ask ourselves why textiles and sectors of export interest to developing countries are the most prone to environmental measures, as the empirical studies of UNCTAD have shown? Could we ask ourselves even more questions, such as:

- Are such measures based on international standards?
- Is there sufficient scientific evidence for their application?
- Are there other measures with similar effects, but less disruptive to trade in textiles from developing countries?

In the light of the additional environmental standards imposed unilaterally, and the apparent back-loading of the implementation of the Agreement on Textiles and Clothing to the final stage, developing exporting countries are becoming more fearful that market entry will become all the more difficult and cumbersome by the time the integration of the textiles and clothing sector in the multilateral trading system takes place after ten years.

I have raised all these questions again, not knowing where they would bring us. Not very far, I assume, as they will be met with opposition and blockage by the developed countries. So how serious is the debate on environment and market access, especially when we see developed countries every day forcing market openings in sectors of interest to them such as telecommunications or technology or financial services, but not in textiles and clothing or agriculture? This should not discourage developing countries from insisting on additional market access offers to promote economic growth in order to improve their capabilities to implement sustainable development, including environmental reforms and better management. I hope we can have the NGOs as close allies in such a debate.

On the other hand, it has been explicitly stressed by the developing countries that they refuse to see environment as an added and new 'conditionality'. Nevertheless, the temptation is great to link market access with environmental performance. Some of the questions would then be: how can we do it in a way that is not discriminatory; can we think of any multilateral disciplines to define what is environmentally friendly; is WTO the right forum? The essence here would be linking additional market access to environmental performance in a non-discriminatory manner, i.e. in a way that ensures that developed countries do not impose their conditions unilaterally.

The relevant provisions of the TRIPS Agreement

Another highly contentious issue that will necessitate considerable work in the future is the relationship between the WTO Agreement on Trade-Related Aspects of Intellectual Property Rights (TRIPS) and the protection of the environment and the promotion of sustainable development. While developing countries do not contest the argument put by the developed countries that stronger intellectual property rights (IPRs) are advantageous for innovation, they argue on their part that stronger IPR regimes – at least in the short run – may have the effect of raising the net costs of acquiring technologies, including environmentally sound technology (ESTs). This issue was raised generally in the CTE last year, but induced hardly any in-depth discussion owing to the very strong resistance put up by the developed countries – i.e. the United States, European Union and Canada – which feared triggering a discussion on the necessity of any modifications to the provisions of the TRIPS Agreement, in particular Article 27.

Future work in this area, as stated in para. 208 of the CTE report, will focus on: (1) facilitating access to and transfer and dissemination of ESTs, and (2) the creation of incentives for the conservation of biological diversity, the sustainable use of its components and the fair and equitable sharing of the benefits arising out of the utilization of genetic resources, including the protection of knowledge, innovations and practices of indigenous and local communities embodying traditional lifestyles relevant to the conservation and sustainable use of biodiversity.

Exports of domestically prohibited goods

I am convinced that this issue is better off in an MEA than being negotiated in the WTO, because the furthest we can get, and the most likely agreement we can reach, in the WTO will not exceed another notification procedure. Would such a decision contribute to better environmental management of domestically prohibited goods? This very sensitive question, in my view, is a 'hands-off' area for the WTO; it is better dealt with in an MEA forum, with the assistance of NGOs, which will be needed. Serious consideration should also be given in this context to the process of developing a comprehensive convention on prior informed consent being undertaken by UNEP.

Conclusion

From this brief account, one can see that the future debate on the interface between trade and environment is going to continue well into the future, focusing on institutional as well as substantive matters. On the institutional aspects, the question to be raised is: will such an issue, which is highly interlinked and interrelated, continue to be dealt with in a fragmented manner between UNCTAD, UNEP, CSD, WTO and the World Bank? Cannot the international community decide on 'who does what' with a view to achieving better coordination and better results? For it seems to me that it would be difficult to conceive of any change in the near future on the multiplicity of institutions dealing with the issue, admitting that everyone has their part to play.

On the substantive matters, as UNCTAD has rightly put it, the prevailing perception is that mutual understanding between trade, environment and development communities is still evolving, and that a larger consensus still needs to be forged on a common agenda to strengthen positive synergies and the mutual supportiveness of trade, environment and development. That will have to focus, as I mentioned earlier, on issues such as:

1. cooperative solutions in dealing with global and transboundary environmental problems away from unilateralism and extraterritoriality in the framework of the relationship between MEAs and the WTO.
2. the use of discriminatory trade measures against non-parties to an MEA and, in this context, drawing up a possible definition for MEAs, and moving away from continuing to speculate on whether any modifications to the provisions of the multilateral trading system are required.
3. a multilateral framework for criteria for the use of trade measures for environmental reasons. Such an issue is, however, most controversial. Environmentalists will certainly continue to ask, if there is more than one solution and several are needed to address an issue, how anybody can determine what is 'necessary' and what is not. Yet, if we want to keep the trade regime with its focus on efficiency and seeking the least trade-distorting solutions to the problems, and if the environmentalists accept that integrating the environment within the multilateral trading system is a legitimate trade-related problem, they will have to abide by the prevailing criteria of necessity, efficiency, proportionality and least trade-restrictiveness. The GATT/WTO regime will have to respond to the environment, as it has been in its tradition to respond. It will have to reduce issues to their technical core, to affirm a limited number of principles and to apply them as consistently as possible. Environment cannot be made an exception to the rule.
4. the issue of ecolabelling and the conflicting PPMs within the WTO competence.

The same is true for all other issues: the essence of the future debate on the relationship between trade and environment in the WTO will have to remain how to accommodate the environment without having to alter the very basis of the multilateral trading system. As UNCTAD has rightly put it, the debate will need to consider how to build on the potential synergies between trade liberalization and improved management of the environment through what it may generate from market openings in terms of additional resources to combat poverty, while countering the fears that trade liberalization will lead to the competitive deregulation of standards. This will strengthen the emerging confidence already apparent between the trade, environment and development communities.

So far we have witnessed the debate being driven by the agenda of the developed countries. Developing countries have been late-comers in this very complex and multifaceted relationship between environment and trade. They have shown and proved their interest and, even more, their engagement in the protection of the environment. What they have constantly argued against is the inclination of some to use environment as a protectionist device. Nevertheless, if at some time in the future they have to sit at the negotiating table where the real horse-trading takes place, there must be something significant and meaningful for them there.

5.4 OECD perspective
Michael Reiterer

The OECD Joint Session of Trade and Environment Experts began meeting in 1991. This joint approach has been a strength of the institution, but it is now necessary to work out what to focus on in the next two years. This will be a difficult time, both for the OECD and the WTO. The next WTO Ministerial Conference, due in 1998, will be largely 'ceremonial', marking the 50th anniversary of the GATT. And the WTO agenda is itself very wide.

The OECD Joint Session can choose between as many as 30 topics, but it has to concentrate on just a few. The following principles should help to guide us.

1. An interdisciplinary approach should be adopted:
    (a) using the interdisciplinary work going on in the OECD itself (synergies);
    (b) using the presence of both trade and environment experts in the Joint Session (pooled knowledge);
    (c) using the input of other international organizations present as observers or invited participants.

2. Complementarity with the work of other international fora should be
    ensured in order to avoid duplication, concentrating scarce resources.
    Use should be made of studies and data already available in other fora
    as well as of studies already undertaken in the life of the Joint Session
    but not fully appreciated yet.
3. Experts at the OECD can do the necessary *analytical work*, which is
    less well carried out in a negotiating situation, such as when working
    on a concrete MEA or when discussing issues at the WTO. This think-
    tank function can be encouraged by using the already well-established
    exchange of views with environmental and industrial NGOs. Similarly,
    reflections do not have to be limited to the legal framework of the WTO
    system – though a certain relevance of the topics discussed to the CTE
    agenda is of course needed to fulfil the think-tank function successfully.

Bearing this in mind, I present the following ideas for a future work programme.

New issues

The *Polluter Pays Principle* was originally developed by the OECD, but the
principle needs re-examination in the light of new economic instruments, in
particular the grant or removal of subsidies (e.g. green box, subsidies exception).

The use of *economic instruments*, especially border tax adjustment and
other financial instruments ('greening tax systems'), is important, and
much of the existing analytical work was carried out in the 1970s. Which
instruments, for example, will be foreseen by the Climate Convention? A
case study on the trade of energy resources and the environment could be
the appropriate means to discuss financial instruments as well as resource
implications at the same time.

The trade and environmental implications of *life-cycle management* on
international trade is important in the areas of ecolabelling, PPMs,
packaging, recycling and so on. Here we can cross the bridge of discussing
issues of sovereignty – because sovereignty has lost a lot of importance in
the area of the environment.

The OECD would be a good place to discuss the issue of *how to incorporate
important environmental concepts* such as the precautionary principle into

the multilateral trading system – including the promotion of sustainable consumption and production patterns through economic instruments such as ecolabelling systems and so on. This topic is related to the more general item of the further development of a conceptual framework putting trade and environment into a sustainable development perspective.

The implication of *'green' government procurement policies* on the trading system, and continuation of the analysis of *trade in services and the environment* are both important subjects; tourism is another candidate for a case study after completion of the current transport study.

The built-in agenda of the present work programme of the Joint Session

The existing work of the Joint Session will continue in some areas. This includes:

- *the use of trade measures for environmental purposes:* synthesizing the discussion of the three conventions analysed (Montreal Protocol, CITES, Basel) in order to evaluate the actual trade implications of these MEAs;
- *trade liberalization and the environment:* international trade in services and the environment: synthesizing the discussion on the transport/ freight papers on the situation in America and Europe, and possibly linking up with regulatory reform work;
- *use of economic instruments for environmental purposes:* final reading of the paper on ecolabelling;
- *continuation of the monitoring of activities of:*
  - *other OECD bodies* (with special emphasis on work done by other committees of the OECD in order to ensure a coherent approach; this item includes topics like the Multilateral Agreement on Investment, trade in agricultural products and the environment, development aspects and the environment, the repercussions of the globalization process on the multilateral trading system and the environment);
  - *other international organizations*, such as WTO, UNCTAD, UNDP, CSD and UNEP;
  - *negotiating of MEAs*, either new ones or the further development of existing ones.

In conclusion, I believe that the Joint Session has made a valuable contribution to the trade and environment work, not only in substance but in bringing the two communities closer together around one table.

5.5 UNEP perspective
Hussein Abaza

UNEP's Governing Council at its 19th Session emphasized the role of UNEP in the trade–environment–development debate. To enforce and strengthen UNEP's work in this area and refocus it so that it can provide a balanced and integrated approach to environment, trade and development, it was found prudent to integrate and closely link UNEP's economics and trade programmes.

The main objectives of the new economics, trade and environment programme are:

1. to further the development and implementation of environmental economic tools (assessment and incentives) and analysis as effective means for promoting the integration of environmental considerations in projects, sectoral planning and macroeconomic policies, programmes and plans;
2. to analyse the impacts of integrating environmental considerations in development planning and decision-making, particularly as it affects trade and competitiveness, taking into account the concerns of developing countries and countries in transition to market economies (CITs);
3. to promote efforts that lead to making trade and environment mutually supportive as a necessary prerequisite to formulating sustainable trade and development policies;
4. to enhance the understanding of the effectiveness of the use of trade measures in MEAs on the achievement of environmental goals and on trade and competitiveness of developing countries and CITs;
5. to enhance the understanding of the environmental impact of trade policies and agreements;
6. to support and build institutional capacity in the environmental

assessment of trade policies, taking into account the special needs of developing countries and CITs;

7. to introduce necessary instruments and mechanisms, including technology transfer, market access, finance and capacity building, in order to support efforts leading to the internalization of environmental costs;

8. to contribute to international efforts to promote and facilitate environmentally responsible investments within the financial service sector.

In order to achieve the objectives of the programme, UNEP, with the assistance of an international working group on environment and trade (to be established), including WTO, UNCTAD, World Bank, UNDP, ITC, OECD, CSD, IUCN, WWF, IISD, etc., will undertake work to provide empirical evidence on the following:

1. the effectiveness of trade instruments in MEAs (CITES, Montreal Protocol, Basel Convention) and their economic impacts, as well as more generally the use of trade measures to address global and transboundary environmental problems;

2. environmental impacts of trade policies and agreements, including case studies on the impact of changes in consumption patterns on developing countries, and the impact of structural adjustment programmes and trade liberalization policies;

3. trade implications of various fiscal and market-based instruments, including green taxes, charges, tradeable permits, labelling and certification schemes, deposit-refund systems and packaging and recycling requirements;

4. promotion of awareness and consensus-building for practitioners, policy-makers and the public, and enhancement of the dialogue between trade, environment and economic ministries;

5. the development and enhancement of the capacity of countries in developing and implementing sustainable trade and environmental policies through the convening of national and regional workshops and seminars, preparation and publications of case studies and training material and exchange of information;

6. the development of practical approaches for environmental cost

internalization, bearing in mind their trade implications, particularly on developing countries and CITs; this includes addressing issues related to access to markets, technology and finance, as well as aid and debt issues.

In implementing this integrated environmental economics and trade sub-programme, UNEP will work closely with WTO, UNCTAD, World Bank, UNDP, OECD, ITC, WWF, IUCN and other relevant governmental and non-governmental institutions, in order to ensure synergy and complementarity between UNEP's work and the work undertaken by these institutions. UNEP will work closely with national governments in order to ensure that their environmental as well as developmental concerns are taken into account.

5.6 The CTE: a renewed mandate for change or more dialogue?[87]
James Cameron

In terms of new rules, innovative recommendations or solutions to complex policy conflicts, the Committee on Trade and Environment (CTE) has failed to deliver. The decision directing the first meeting of the General Council of the World Trade Organization to establish a Committee on Trade and Environment, whose purpose would be to undertake a comprehensive review and formulate recommendations in relation to trade and environment measures, was welcomed by most of those concerned about the awkward relationship between trade policy and environmental policy. The decision to establish the Committee resulted indirectly from pressure mounted by environmental nongovernmental organizations, and by the European Parliament negotiating team in the Uruguay Round keeping environment 'on the table'. This turned out to be an indicator of a

---

[87] This paper was originally presented to the National Wildlife Federation, Berkeley Roundtable on International Economy (BRIE), The Council on Foreign Relations and the Nautilus Institute for Sustainable Development, Washington DC, March 1997. It was written by James Cameron and Karen Campbell (a qualified lawyer who has worked in the area of environmental law and policy in Canada for a number of years).

genuine desire to have greater clarity and measurable policy progress on trade and environment issues which was reflected in the policy proposals presented to the CTE by the European Union.

Among other things, the task of the CTE was 'to make appropriate recommendations on whether any modifications of the provisions of the multilateral trading system are required' to ensure a positive interaction between trade and environment measures and policies.[88] Environment and trade experts saw the creation of this Committee as a mechanism by which important issues of environment and trade policy could be comprehensively examined for the first time. Given this scope of the mandate, the potential for the CTE to provide clarity on these issues and make effective recommendations was significant.

In retrospect, perhaps the CTE's agenda was too broad. The Report, tabled at the Ministerial Conference of the WTO in Singapore in December 1996, can be viewed primarily as a summary of issues, not an agenda for change. While the CTE has introduced an element of greater clarity in terms of issue definition, it has done little to bring about concrete action in ensuring a reconciliation or balance between trade and environment issues. The Report's basic conclusions are threefold: that no real modifications to the multilateral trading system are required; that some procedural modifications in terms of transparency and notification should be made; and that the work of the WTO in building a constructive policy relationship between trade, environment and sustainable development should continue.

This last conclusion is perhaps the only measure of comfort that trade and environment experts may garner from the Report, as a window for substantive change to the WTO with respect to environmental policy remains. Given this background, it is timely to analyse the work of the CTE and to identify key considerations which the CTE must address more effectively for their work to make real policy progress on trade-related environmental issues.

---

[88] Decision to establish a Committee on Trade and the Environment, Marrakesh, 15 April 1994.

Context

The period since the Rio Summit in 1992 and the signing of the Uruguay Round Agreement in Marrakesh in 1994 has seen unprecedented developments in both world trade and global environmental issues. This dynamic is unlikely to slow in the near future, and this paper is therefore premissed on the belief that the work of the CTE will be highly significant (although not exclusively so) in shaping the formation of trade and environment-related policy, both globally and domestically, in the years to come.[89] The following analysis will focus on critical areas of the work of the CTE, noting missed opportunities and making recommendations for future discussion on outstanding issues. This review is focused on areas of primary concern, and does not purport to undertake a comprehensive review of each of the ten agenda items in the Report. Further, given this broad perspective, the comments that follow are put in the context of the role of the WTO, and are of relevance to anyone considering trade-related environment matters generally.

Any examination of the linkages between the WTO and environmental protection must be framed upon the assumption that the WTO is one organ in the body of public international law. To date, the general perception of many delegates and secretariat personnel has been that the GATT and the WTO function independently from public international law. Indeed, the CTE Report makes limited reference to the role of international law in the interpretation of the GATT.[90] This qualification is critical in that it clarifies that the GATT and its related agreements, while specialized, are not derived from a separate legal order, and must be interpreted in the light of principles and practices operative of public international law.

---

[89] For example, there are currently at least four critical negotiation processes under way which have implications for trade and the environment, including the ongoing work of the CTE: the UNEP/FAO efforts to establish a Prior Informed Consent Convention for trade in chemicals and pesticides; amendments to the 1989 Basel Convention on Transboundary Movements of Hazardous Waste; ongoing amendments to CITES; and the work of the Intergovernmental Panel on Forests at the Commission for Sustainable Development.

[90] *Report of the Committee on Trade and Environment*, WT/CTE/1 (12 November 1996), para. 15 does note that 'MEAs and the WTO both represent different bodies of international law'.

This assumption has been verified by the Appellate Body of the WTO in its 1996 Report regarding Standards for Reformulated and Conventional Gasoline.[91] In applying the Vienna Convention on the Law of Treaties to the GATT and other 'covered agreements' of the WTO, it states that 'the General Agreement is not to be read in clinical isolation from public international law'.[92] Indeed, the Appellate Body's ruling that the GATT must be interpreted within the corpus of public international law leads to the inevitable implication that the environmental principles derived from sources of international law will form part of the jurisprudence of the WTO.[93]

Role of non-state actors

To date, there has been insufficient scope for non-state actors such as nongovernmental organizations, including environmental groups and industry associations, and intergovernmental organizations (IGOs) to participate in the work of the CTE. Item 10 of the CTE Report addresses the role of intergovernmental and nongovernmental organizations in relation to the work of the WTO. Despite recognizing that WTO members have agreed 'to improve public access to WTO documentation and to develop communication with NGOs',[94] the Report's recommendations do little to give real effect to this commitment.

---

[91] *Report of the Appellate Body, United States – Standards for Reformulated and Conventional Gasoline*, WT/DS2/AB/R (29 April 1996).
[92] Ibid., p.17.
[93] The further significance of this development is that the GATT interpretation will be broadened to consider general international legal principles, including international environmental law principles, relevant to a trade dispute. The associated result is that future analyses of Article XX of the GATT will be extended to include general environmental principles as well. Therefore, serious consideration should be given to amendment of Article XX, as its de facto amendment will be inevitable. See further discussion of Article XX, *infra*.
[94] *Report of the Committee on Trade and Environment*, para. 214.

NGOs

The focus of the recommendations with respect to NGOs is primarily on notification and communication in the WTO and CTE, not necessarily on improved access and transparency. The CTE has recommended that all remaining working documents prepared during its first two years of operations be derestricted, and that the WTO Secretariat 'continue its interaction with NGOs which will contribute to the accuracy and richness of the public debate on trade and environment'.[95] The CTE's recommendations with respect to NGO access, while minimal, do represent progress on this important issue.

However, it is imperative that in its continued work the CTE provide appropriate access to NGOs throughout its deliberations. One notable omission is that, while the CTE recommends that past documentation be derestricted, it makes no reference to the derestriction of working papers for the next round of deliberations concurrent with their discussion at the CTE. In our view, current information, and not simply previous documentation, should be derestricted and made available for public access and comment. Moreover, the burden in the WTO's policy on access to documentation should be shifted to provide unrestricted access to all documents unless there is a clear and convincing reason why this should not apply. Increased transparency can only aid in a wider consideration of issues and potential solutions.

The need to open the deliberations of the CTE to greater scrutiny and participation must be emphasized, not least because there is much that the NGO community can offer the WTO regarding non-state actor access. Despite some arguments that the GATT and now WTO have functioned effectively in regulating international trade for the past fifty years, this initial purely trade-driven paradigm no longer exists. The mere existence of the CTE speaks to the interdisciplinary nature of global policy development. The CTE's initial failure to provide access to its documentation caused international attention to be focused on the inaccessibility of the WTO generally, and NGO pressure for access to better information has led the WTO to improve access to all areas of its work, not simply trade

---

[95] Ibid., paras. 216, 217.

and environment. In focusing attention on broader issues, many organizations reflecting different interests are now benefiting from the changes championed by environmental NGOs.

A similar concern exists with regard to observer status at CTE meetings. While the CTE has agreed to extend observer status on a permanent basis to IGOs that previously participated as observers on an ad hoc basis, this concession has not been extended to NGOs.[96] NGOs were granted observer status at the Ministerial Conference in Singapore, a significant and welcome change to the status quo. Although there was not a great deal of activity for them to undertake in respect of arguments for change, their presence was largely constructive. The Singapore government's initiative in publicizing NGO activities at the Ministerial Conference was a notable gesture in favour of cooperation with non-state actors.

Indeed, experience to date in various fora indicates that NGOs bring fresh perspectives which ultimately enhance consideration of policy issues. Both the WTO and the CTE are still in stages of relative institutional infancy, and there is much that NGOs can contribute to the effective operation and development of the WTO in terms of evaluating and commenting on the difficult issues it will be called upon to consider. NGO experience brings with it not only a frequently different perspective, but also new information, hands-on expertise, the ability to represent interests not otherwise considered in state-to-state diplomacy, and a more immediate appreciation of issues of public concern. In sum, there is no good reason for denying NGOs access as observers to the CTE, particularly given the precedent set in Singapore. Rules and conditions of access could be drafted easily.

IGOs

Another important element of non-state actor participation is the role of IGOs at the CTE. Experience in the first two years has indicated that there is a clear need for enhanced institutional cooperation at the CTE. For example, organizations such as UNEP and UNCTAD cannot be heard in

---

[96] Ibid., para. 217.

the CTE without the invitation of a country delegate. Practice has so far
not extended this courtesy, even though the Committee could benefit from
contributions by these organizations. Unfortunately, attempts to bring
UNEP and UNCTAD together on the trade, environment and development
policy nexus have not been altogether successful to date – the October
1996 Ministerial Conference in Geneva is a case in point. This raises a
larger question about the effectiveness of the international environmental
institutions. The trade and environment debate has revealed the relative
weakness of UNEP in the face of the WTO and the urgent need of a more
coherent resonant voice for sustainable development at the global level.
None of the institutions we currently have can play this role. The system
for the institutional management of global environment and development
affairs is fractured; the WTO, despite flaws and its own financial worries,
is not.

Multilateral environmental agreements and the WTO

The main issues concerning multilateral environmental agreements (MEAs)
and the multilateral trading system are twofold: reconciling trade-related
environmental measures between the WTO and MEAs, and choosing a
forum for the settlement of a trade-related environmental dispute. Although
these were separate agenda items, the overlap was such that the CTE Report
presents its conclusions on these issues together. Overall, the Report's
comments with respect to MEAs amount to little more than a recognition
of the critical relationship between MEAs and the multilateral trading
system, and their comments on this important issue are inconclusive and,
at best, persuasive. Given the complexity of the issues, it is extremely
disappointing that the CTE's only actual recommendation on these two
key issues is 'that the WTO Secretariat continue to play a constructive role
through its cooperative efforts with Secretariats of MEAs and provide
information to WTO Members on trade-related work in MEAs'.[97]

On these issues we limit ourselves, on this occasion, to two *a priori*
comments. First, we advocate a more definitive approach to situations

---

[97] Ibid., para. 175.

where a dispute looms regarding a trade-related environmental measure enacted pursuant to an MEA. Second, we examine the broader issue of the effectiveness of the dispute settlement mechanism in the WTO, for both environment and other disputes, providing considerations for possible reform.

Disputes and Article XX

The CTE's work in this area amounts primarily to a recognition that, where parties to an MEA agree to apply a specifically mandated trade measure, disputes over the application of such measures are unlikely to occur in the WTO.[98] Further, the Report recognizes that, to date, no parties have resorted to the WTO Dispute Settlement Mechanism to undermine obligations accepted in becoming parties to an MEA, and it 'considers this will remain the case'.[99] This is precarious reasoning for failing to make explicit recommendations on the reconciliation of disputes that arise in the context of both the WTO and an MEA. Furthermore, the Report's statement that in the event of a dispute parties should try to resolve the matter through the dispute settlement mechanisms of the MEA falls conspicuously short of a recommendation even if we agree with its sense.[100] Disputes will inevitably arise, playing off trade-related environmental measures in MEAs against the provisions of the WTO. The CTE's tactic of willing the issue to go away implies that it has, perhaps deliberately, failed to make a recommendation on an issue that will probably become contentious at some point. It may be hoped that the Appellate Body would treat such contentious disputes with more respect for international law than a GATT panel using Article XX, but it would have been nice to give them some tools to work with.

Despite not making an explicit recommendation to this effect, the language of the Report clearly reflects the view that in the event of a conflict dispute settlement mechanisms in MEAs should take precedence over the WTO. It is unfortunate that the CTE failed to turn this view into a

---

[98] Ibid., para. 174 (iv).
[99] Ibid., para. 178.
[100] Ibid., para. 178.

recommendation, particularly where the states involved in a dispute are both parties to the MEA and member states of the WTO. As the House of Commons Select Committee on World Trade and the Environment notes, 'successful negotiation and implementation of multilateral environmental agreements is a vital element in tackling global and transboundary environmental problems'.[101] Undermining measures inspired by such agreements, by making them subject to the often contrary policy goals of the WTO, will frustrate MEAs and the pressing goals of global environmental protection generally. Further, if, as the CTE believes, it will be 'the case' that no disputes regarding the implementation of environmental measures under a MEA will be subject to the WTO dispute mechanism, then explicitly providing that a MEA will prevail should be of little political consequence; indeed, it ought to be a non-issue.

Yet another reason for clarifying whether MEA disputes will prevail over the WTO stems from consideration of the international law of treaties. This law provides general rules which could be interpreted such that in some instances MEA provisions will prevail over those of the WTO. The issue in this case would be one of characterization – should the dispute in question be framed as a trade dispute or an environmental dispute? It is clear that trade disputes should be addressed by the WTO. However, in many cases the characterization of disputes over trade-related environmental measures will be very different, and may warrant favouring the application of the relevant provisions of the MEA over those of the WTO. While this argument has not been judicially tested, it remains worthy of consideration.[102]

Furthermore, the General Exceptions in Article XX of the GATT contain ample protection against measures that could be viewed as arbitrary or unjustifiably discriminatory or as disguised restrictions on trade. That no trade-related environmental measure has ever passed the test to benefit

---

[101] House of Commons, Session 1995–6, Environment Committee, 4th Report, *World Trade and the Environment* (Cm 149, June 1996), Vol. I, para. 187.
[102] For a further discussion, see James Cameron and Jonathan Robinson, 'The Use of Trade Provisions in International Environmental Agreements and their Compatibility with the GATT', *Yearbook of International Environmental Law*, 2 (London: Graham & Trotman, 1991).

from the exceptions in Article XX evidences this fact. Indeed, the Appellate Body's ruling in the Gasoline case (see Section 4.3 above) further elaborates the Article XX test, giving greater credence to the chapeau in ensuring against abuse of the General Exception provisions. In discussing the two-tiered approach to analysis of Article XX (justification of the measure under the listed exceptions, and further appraisal of the same measure under the chapeau), the Appellate Body states that 'it is important to underscore that the purpose and object of the introductory clauses of Article XX is generally the prevention of 'abuse of the exceptions'.[103] The Appellate Body specifies further that 'the provisions of the chapeau cannot logically refer to the same standard(s) by which a violation of a substantive rule has been determined to have occurred. To proceed down that path would be both to empty the chapeau of its contents and to deprive the exceptions in paragraphs (a) to (j) of meaning.'[104] This two-tiered approach elaborated by the Appellate Body for Article XX makes clear that measures that could be perceived as abuses of the exceptions stand a minimal chance of passing the rigorous test for protection under Article XX.

In our view, then, there is a explicit need to clarify how (against what principles) specific provisions of MEAs, or measures chosen by parties to implement obligations in MEAs, will be considered in WTO dispute settlement. This clarification can easily be accomplished through simple amendment to Article XX of the GATT. Draft wording was developed by the European Commission and tabled on behalf of the European Union and its member states, before the CTE at its meeting in February 1996.[105] The need for articulated ground rules is clear; this is a view shared by

---

[103] *Report of the Appellate Body – Standards for Reformulated and Conventional Gasoline*, p. 22.

[104] Ibid., p. 23.

[105] The proposal contained the following two options for amending Article XX:

    (1) Add an additional paragraph (k) with an Understanding to be agreed between WTO Members [draft Understanding was included as Annex A to the proposal]. Paragraph (k) to read:

        (k) taken pursuant to a MEA complying with the provisions of the Understanding on the relationship between MEA-based measures and the WTO rules.

such disparate interests as Greenpeace, the UK House of Commons Select Committee on the Environment, and the US Council for International Business. To advance no recommendation for the amendment of Article XX was the CTE's plainest failure.

Dispute settlement mechanisms

The approach of the CTE on this issue also has been inadequate thus far, and there are several avenues for further consideration. The following suggestions are offered up not only for the consideration of the CTE in its renewed mandate, but also in the context of the forthcoming four-year review of the WTO Dispute Settlement Understanding (DSU).

Experience with the first two years of the DSU leads to some interesting considerations about the future role of dispute settlement within the WTO. There is little doubt that dispute resolution is increasingly becoming a core function of the WTO, and that more resources will be committed to balancing the interests of members in the context of disputes or potential disputes. This is not surprising, given the number and complexity of agreements administered by the WTO, and the vast diversity of contracting parties' interests. In this context, the role of the Appellate Body will become more critical in interpreting these agreements and balancing interests of members in such a way that it is conceivable that the focus of the WTO will shift away from panel proceedings and towards the work of the Appellate Body.

Given that the role of the DSU will become more critical in the WTO, it is essential that consideration be given to improving the WTO's ability to adjudicate effectively on trade and trade-related matters. It is notable that the CTE did not even explore potential mechanisms for improving the functioning of the Dispute Settlement Body in the context of trade and environment disputes. While our primary interest is in ensuring that

---

(2) Amend paragraph (b) to read:

  (b) necessary to protect human, animal, plant life or health or the environment; and measures taken pursuant to Multilateral Environmental Agreements complying with the provisions of the 'Understanding on the relationship between MEA-based trade measures and the WTO rules' (Annex A).

environmental policy issues are given adequate consideration in the context of trade disputes, a review of new approaches to dispute resolution is equally valuable for the resolution of disputes on other subject areas as well. The following four recommendations, sadly all made before in some form or other, are offered as mechanisms to enhance both trust and participation in WTO dispute resolution.

1. *Appointment of Counsel to the Panel.* The European Court of Justice model might be considered in any review of the DSU, as its structure and approach have much to offer the WTO. Specifically, consideration should be given to the appointment of an Advocate General or Counsel to the Panel, whose role would be to either supplement or, more radically, supplant the role of the Panel. In the European Court of Justice, the Advocate General's function is similar to that of Counsel to the Court. The Advocate General summarizes the submissions of the parties, and makes recommendations as to where the Court should focus its efforts, and as to how the legal issues should be resolved. Notably, the scope of the Advocate General's authority is not limited to merely summarizing and presenting the submissions of the parties; he or she is also entitled to submit any other arguments which may be relevant to the Court's determination.

   The application of this concept in the context of WTO dispute settlement would mean that there would be an Advocate General, functioning as an independent agent either to the Panel or, more ideally, to the Appellate Body, positioned to inform the adjudicator, in an even-handed way, on relevant GATT and related law, including international law.

2. *Establishment of a right of intervention.* Provision for the submission of *amicus curiae* briefs, or non-state interventions, should be incorporated into the DSU. This right of intervention, in either the panel system or the Appellate Body, would allow an interested person or group to present evidence and argumentation to the Panel or Appellate Body. Initially, this right could be made available in the form of written briefs, on the basis of a sufficient interest test, and theoretically it could be extended as full disputing party rights to persons or

groups with a sufficient interest in the dispute. This concept is also compatible with the role of Counsel to the Panel.

As stated earlier, there is much that the NGO community can offer the WTO, both in terms of general policy direction and in the context of specific disputes. NGO expertise, knowledge and insight would clearly enhance decision-making and adjudication of panels and the Appellate Body. Equally, most disputes that come before panels are disputes between corporations or corporation agreements about access to markets. Let us hear corporations present their private interests distinct from the public interests of the state.

3. Provision for increased access to information. Related to the notion of non-state intervention is the extension of a general right to information regarding disputes. Access to all documents should be unrestricted unless there is a clear and convincing reason why they should not be available. This right would include timely public access to submissions relating to disputes, official reports, digests of cases and pending results. The policy reasons for this recommendation are substantially the same as above – greater transparency will provide for more fulsome assessment and adjudication of the issues.

4. Advisory options from the International Court of Justice. Finally, the Panel or Appellate Body should have the power to seek advisory opinions from the International Court of Justice (ICJ) on matters of international law, as was intended by the drafters of the Havana Charter.[106] Situations, in particular those pertaining to environmental measures, will inevitably arise where GATT panels do not have the necessary expertise to advocate on highly specialized fact situations. Reference to an independent panel such as the ICJ would attest to the impartiality of the WTO in the resolution of trade-related disputes. In addition, such references to the ICJ could supplement an amendment to Article XX of the GATT, discussed earlier.[107]

---

[106] The Havana Charter for an International Trade Organization was drafted between 1946 and 1948, but it never entered into force.

[107] For a more detailed discussion of possible reforms to the WTO, see James Cameron and Zen Makuch, *Sustainable Development and Integrated Dispute Settlement in GATT 1994*, WWF International Discussion Paper (1994).

Paradoxically, the above recommendations would have the effect of judicializing the WTO at a time when domestic courts and tribunals seem to be moving towards less adversarial methods of dispute resolution. However, changes such as those proposed will be essential to maintain the integrity and impartiality of the WTO dispute settlement system. The nature and diversity of interests in the multilateral trading system are such that clear legal approaches are the best way to protect against abuse of power and the impartial distribution of trade rights and obligations.

Process and production methods

The issue of process and production methods (PPMs) was reviewed in item 3(b), in the context of measures relating to products. The main focus of the CTE's work is concern about the trade implications of voluntary ecolabelling schemes, and its failure to deal adequately with either PPMs or ecolabelling is evidenced by the fact that it made no recommendations at all on either matter. This result is wholly unsatisfactory. Conclusions on this issue are brief and based upon the discussion in the Report.[108]

It appears that there is no political agreement on whether to tolerate PPM-based measures. Given that this issue has formed the basis for highly contentious panel decisions in the past, this is clearly an area in which the CTE should have made definitive recommendations. It should not be that difficult to develop a series of considerations for the evaluation of the nature and impact of PPMs as indirect barriers to trade. Effective approaches to dealing with the issue are simple. If there are global or transboundary effects to a PPM, the first-best response will be international cooperation, the development of multilateral agreements or harmonization. If the effect of the PPM is local or domestic, the first-best response will be domestic regulation. It should not be presumed that states will regulate the local environmental effects of their domestic PPMs.

However, there are a host of PPMs in a variety of sectors that do cause transboundary or global effects, and there are real problems with the

---

[108] *Report of the Committee on Trade and Environment*, paras. 61–73.

enforcement of domestic environmental law designed to deal with the local environmental effects of PPMs. For these reasons, it is essential that some basic ground rules be drafted to guide environmental regulators in the exercise of their duties to protect the environment in a globalized economy.

Quite another issue is that which arises when PPMs so affect the product itself that an environmental or health issue crosses a border with a product. In that situation, Article XX already provides reasonable protection to the importing state, but it would be helpful if it were made absolutely clear that the environmental effects of traded goods or services were covered by Article XX.

Ecolabelling

As mentioned above, since the CTE made no recommendations under this item, it is clear that no real solutions have been proposed. This is extremely disappointing, given the scope of the CTE's consideration of the trade implications of voluntary ecolabelling schemes. The CTE's comments on this item reflect a desire to ensure transparency in the preparation, adoption and application of such schemes, and in ensuring fair access to foreign producers for such programmes. Their only position on this issue is that WTO members follow the provisions of the Technical Barriers to Trade (TBT) Agreement and its Code of Good Practice.

There is clearly a need for more substantive work to be undertaken on this matter, and for a set of procedures and substantive principles to be developed. Ecolabelling schemes are an important way of increasing consumer awareness and altering production practices in the market place. Continued development of these schemes should be encouraged, even though we know that ecolabels create market segmentation and have the capacity to create market distortions. Additionally, the basic ground rules for PPMs would apply here. Increasing access to the labelling process for exporters is one good way of helping to avoid conflicts, but it seems inevitable that these conflicts will continue and may find their way to WTO dispute settlement. A challenge to the EC Ecolabel with its multi-criteria life-cycle approach now seems inevitable. The frustration is that the DSU today has no more assistance from the CTE as to how it should settle this dispute than it had two years ago.

Domestically prohibited goods

Item 7 of the CTE Report addresses the issue of exports of domestically prohibited goods (DPGs). The CTE accurately acknowledges that the export of DPGs is of primary concern to developing and least developed countries, and that trade in potentially hazardous or harmful products is being addressed by a variety of different IGOs. As with most other agenda items, the CTE's real contribution is to acknowledge the importance of the issue and then to recommend greater information sharing and more research. In this case the CTE's two recommendations on DPGs pertain to greater cooperation with IGOs working on this issue, and further research by the WTO Secretariat.[109]

In our view, further research and information sharing will do little to resolve the reality that developing countries cannot adequately protect themselves against exported hazardous DPGs. Several MEAs already establish rules governing the shipment and disposal of DPGs, and there are a number of voluntary guidelines in place to ensure informed consent prior to the disposal of such goods.[110] Therefore, developing rules is not the answer. The real issue is the practical one of financing to ensure that a prior informed consent system could be implemented effectively. Thus, CTE efforts should be focused on developing financing mechanisms, as developing countries often do not have the resources to monitor their borders and fully inform themselves, leaving them unable to protect themselves against exported DPGs. Current intergovernmental efforts to develop a Prior Informed Consent (PIC) Convention may assist developing

---

[109] Ibid., paras. 201 and 203 respectively.

[110] The Basel Convention on the Transboundary Movements of Hazardous Waste has provisions governing the shipment of hazardous waste. Similarly, the 'London Guidelines for the Exchange of Information on Chemicals in International Trade' and the Prior Informed Consent procedure establish voluntary procedures for the treatment of DPGs (both pertain only to chemicals).

countries in this regard.[111] Of course, a successfully negotiated PIC Convention with wide membership would become an MEA and should be treated as such in the WTO. The CTE's next steps on the issue of DPGs should be to work within the WTO and with other IGOs to develop a system of financing for developing countries to identify and reject shipments of hazardous materials.

Market access

As with PPMs and ecolabelling, the CTE made no recommendations on this issue of market access for exporters in item 6. Aside from assessing the nature of the concern, the CTE then suggested that its analysis should be broadened to include sectors other than agriculture and energy. The key concern in this regard is restricted market access for exporting countries, which has the effect of discouraging sustainable development. Measures such as tariff escalations, quotas and domestic production subsidies often result in trade barriers which can have a negative effect on development and on the environment in exporting countries.[112] These protective measures are often applied to protect natural-resource-based industries such as coal production and forest management, which cause environmental degradation. The net result of restricted market access is that it prohibits access not only to markets, but also to environmental technology and the development of technical goods and services which could provide for the more sustainable use and management of such resources.

As with other agenda items, simple policy recommendations seem to have eluded the CTE in this area as well. To ensure that restricted market access does not result in unnecessary environmental degradation, a systematic evaluation of such trade barriers should be undertaken with a view to characterizing their intended and unintended effects. In situations where trade barriers have the effect of prohibiting the flow of goods and services which can enhance environmental protection, such barriers

---

[111] Negotiations for a draft PIC Convention, covering trade in chemicals and pesticides, were completed in March 1998, and the final text will be signed later in the year.
[112] For a useful discussion of market access, see 'Expert Panel on Trade and Sustainable Development: Report of First Meeting' (Gland, Switzerland: WWF, October, 1996).

should be removed. Free access to information and technology can only assist in the development of creative solutions, which, in many cases, the private sector is becoming increasingly well positioned to provide.

Conclusions

The overwhelming sense one has from assessing the CTE's work thus far is one of disappointment. In Marrakesh, there was an explicit decision for the CTE to table concrete recommendations to ensure the harmonious development of trade and environment policies. The CTE's focus to date has been merely to characterize issues; and there has been little discussion of substantive issues other than recognizing the status quo. Progress on their real mandate of making recommendations regarding modifications to the multilateral trading system can best be described as glacial. Hopefully, this lost opportunity can be made up with the renewed mandate.

Despite the CTE's failure to develop effective policy solutions to trade and environment matters, thus far its existence has had several, perhaps unintended, benefits. Notably, the creation of the CTE provided new opportunities for NGOs to work together on these issues. Networks such as the Global Environment and Trade Study (GETS) have facilitated conferences, produced working papers and participated in various fora to discuss issues. Similarly, the Policy Dialogue on Trade and the Environment, operated through the Consensus-Building Institute, created a dialogue between the principal players in the trade–environment debate from all sectors, allowing for a free flow of ideas which would not have been possible in more formal arrangements. Yet another example is the Expert Panel on Trade and Sustainable Development, brought together through the World Wide Fund for Nature to develop creative approaches to addressing these issues.

The ongoing work of the CTE also enabled, and indeed will continue to provide for, a series of other NGO networks to be strengthened in large part through the work of the new International Centre for Trade and Sustainable Development. Many more initiatives are under way and good work has been done by a variety of groups, including some excellent reports from the business community (e.g. the World Business Council for Sustainable Development Report on Trade and Environment).

Perhaps the CTE failed because the WTO is still too closely connected in mind and spirit to the GATT. Delegates are uncomfortable at policy-making. Negotiation is understood but all the training and experience is locked on to getting concessions. Policy planning for the avoidance of future conflicts is a different discipline. There is obviously much more work to do to properly integrate environmental policy, trade policy and development policy. We are short of understanding, but we are right to be indignant that so little has been achieved with what we do know in the two and a half years of CTE work.

5.7 Discussion

Much of the discussion focused on the value and future of the CTE. Some participants put forward a highly critical view, regarding the CTE as too politicized to carry out any useful analytical work, and too narrowly focused in its remit to be able to properly integrate all of the concerns of the trade, environment and development communities. It was even suggested that a focus on the CTE actively discouraged useful work from proceeding elsewhere.

In its defence, it was pointed out that the CTE was not, and could not be, an environmental body. It had a specific remit set for it by ministers at Marrakesh – mainly to identify the relationship between environmental measures and the multilateral trading system – and it could not, and did not wish to, extend itself beyond those boundaries. It was felt that the experience of the Committee so far had been beneficial in enabling the exchange of views and contributing to a better understanding of the issues. The belief that there were such things as a fixed 'trade community' and an equally set 'environmental community' was challenged; a former ambassador pointed out that many diplomats were often members of both. The trade–environment debate should be seen not as a 'negotiation' but rather as a 'cooperation'.

As in the discussion following the session on 'industry concerns' (Section 3.5), many speakers stated the case for a single effective Global Environmental Organization. This was seen as desirable for a variety of reasons: to act as a counterweight to the WTO (perhaps with an equivalent

'Committee on Environment and Trade', with regular exchanges of views with the CTE); to carry out effective analytical work and, more to the point, to promote it to policy-makers; and to encourage higher environmental standards world-wide, ideally to the point where trade restrictions designed to enforce them were unnecessary. In the absence of such an organization, an intergovernmental panel was proposed to carry the debate forward at least and to help to integrate the fractured views of the plethora of environment and trade departments, NGOs and IGOs.

One point with which no one disagreed was the need for better coordination of trade and environment policies at national levels. Opening up the debate, and the institutions, to participation by NGOs and industry was also believed to be valuable and constructive. It was accepted that the trade–environment–development debate was still evolving and would continue to do so, and that in the long run, despite the difficulties, it must be possible to reach a positive and mutually supportive relationship between these objectives.

also available ...

Duncan Brack

International Trade and the Montreal Protocol

The Montreal Protocol on Substances that Deplete the Ozone Layer is one of the most effective multilateral environmental agreements currently in existence. Established to control the production and consumption of CFCs and other ozone-depleting chemicals, the Protocol is an important example of an agreement which places restrictions on international trade in the interests of the global environment - a feature which may become common in future treaties.

This report examines the development, effectiveness and future of the trade provisions of the ozone regime, concluding that they have contributed significantly to its success in attracting signatories and in limiting ozone depletion. Issues considered include the compatibility of the trade provisions and the GATT, trade restrictions and developing countries, and the new problems of non-compliance and illegal trade in CFCs.

Duncan Brack is a Senior Research Fellow at the Royal Institute of International Affairs.

Distributed exclusively in the USA and Canada by the Brookings Institution.

1996   RIIA/Earthscan   Price £12.95

Energy and Environmental Programme

THE ROYAL INSTITUTE OF INTERNATIONAL AFFAIRS

John Mitchell (ed.)

Companies in a World of Conflict:

Companies, NGOs and Corporate Responsibility

Globalization is confronting companies with choices that are not simply economic, nor clearly defined within a political 'safe haven' of national or international laws and regulations. In the emerging global civil society there are conflicts of values as well as conflicts of national interests. Governments and international organizations are learning to respond to the pressures of opinion communicated across borders by instant media and transnational NGOs. Companies need to learn to do the same.

This book is an introduction and a guide to this newly developing area of study and action. A distinguished group of academic, business and diplomatic experts describe the mechanisms by which companies are challenged to account for the social as well as the economic consequences of their actions. The chapters provide examples ranging from extraterritorial US sanctions on Iran and Libya, to human rights and the petroleum industry, and the experience of companies responding to public and private sanctions on South Africa during the apartheid regime.

Distributed exclusively in the USA and. Canada by the Brookings Institution

Feb 1998   RIIA/Earthscan   Price £16.95